Lewis Grizzard
The Dawg That Did Not Hunt

Peter Stoddard

- **Print Length:** 482 pages
- **Publication Date:** January 28, 2019
- **Sold by:** Amazon Digital Services LLC
- **Language:** English
- **ISBN:** 9781795440271

Courier font selected as it most closely resembles what Lewis's Remington or Royal typewriter would have cranked out.

Contents

Dedication

For my sons Kevin Stoddard and Ben Stoddard, two of the brightest and funniest human beings on earth.

If only Lewis Grizzard could have enjoyed the joy of fatherhood you have brought to me.

Foreword

In lieu of a traditional foreword, one comment from a key contributor. Then notes on early research.

Celebrated author and journalist Frederick Allen offered this:

"That's got to be the fastest book ever published!"

Frederick did not say it was good. He said it was fast. But he approved his own chapter, so I'll take it.

Notes on early research:

It is 1:17 PM, Monday, October 22, 2018. I sit at the Forsyth County Georgia Public Library with a copy of a posthumous collection of stories written by my literary

hero, the late, great Lewis
Grizzard.

I believe this to be the only
Grizzard book I have not yet read.

This morning I had breakfast with
an interesting person who knew
Lewis well. We agreed that the
world needs a Grizzard revival of
some sort. We do not know what
shape that revival will take. I
aspire to make it happen.

I became vaguely aware of Lewis Grizzard in the 1970s. My parents subscribed to the Atlanta Journal, the evening paper. Grizzard was the Journal's young sports editor, and sports was about the only section that interested pre-teen me.

Lewis then disappeared for a brief and infamous stint in Chicago. Upon his return south in 1977, he quickly transitioned from sports to humor at the Atlanta Constitution, the morning paper. I don't recall if my parents switched their subscription, but I somehow found Grizzard columns.

Lewis Grizzard may be the only reason I read anything but the sports page today.

When he died at age 47 in 1994, Lewis was a nationally famous, and, yes, infamous, syndicated columnist. He was a veteran of

speaking tours, the talk show
circuit and at least one sitcom.

Ironically, I left Atlanta for
Chicago in 1984, and at first
Lewis fell off my radar screen. My
Chicago years were glorious, very
unlike those Lewis so often and
vividly recalled. I read the
Chicago Tribune and Sun Times.
Lewis was not syndicated in
either. I began to read his books.

On visits to Atlanta over the
years I would often lodge with my
now ex-wife in the guest room of
my beloved late ex-father-in-law.
I think Lewis would like that last
sentence. I hope so. On the guest
bathroom counter next to the
throne was a rotating stack of
Lewis Grizzard books.

That gave me the opportunity to
dive into editions I had not seen.
Soon after Lewis's premature
death, my father-in-law hung in

the guest hallway a framed copy of
the cartoon showing Catfish
greeting Lewis at the Pearly Gates
of Heaven. I initially showed that
image here until I concluded it
would be a copyright violation.
Google "lewis at the pearly gates"
to see it. Many people I have met
still have it hanging somewhere.

Lewis set the satire hook deep in
me. In college at our mutually
beloved University of Georgia, I
subscribed to National Lampoon
magazine. I became a voracious
consumer of anything written by
P.J. O'Rourke and other fine
satirists. P.J., you can thank
Lewis for luring me away from the
sports page and indirectly luring
me to you.

But back to Lewis. At breakfast
this morning I learned that many
Grizzard books are no longer in
print. No true biography has ever
been written. There are untold

volumes of stories never told, which is why they qualify as untold. Okay, Lewis would probably sneer at that last sentence.

I like to think I share a few key traits in common with Lewis. I really do not care if anything I write is politically correct. Lewis wrote edgy while using clean language. He had a knack for knowing boundaries. He could take potshots at things and people he did not like without being vulgar or profane.

Newspapers have come full circle. I have zero tolerance for journalistic political correctness. Many days I can't even stomach the sports page.

It is time to commemorate the life and legacy of Lewis Grizzard.

Lewis Grizzard

The Dawg That Did Not Hunt

Restoring the Legacy of America's Greatest Columnist

Peter Stoddard

A Collection of Grizzard Stories
The World Has Never Heard
As Told by Many Who Knew Lewis Best

Introduction

First, yes that photo on the previous book cover is a little awkward. I would prefer that it show me with my arm around Lewis's shoulder like we were pals. But the two dimensional cutout did not allow that. So there.

How does one go about writing a biography of someone who wrote 25 books?

It is not easy, but one thing I chose not to do is reread any of those books to the extent I could help it. If I did that I might find myself writing stuff Lewis already wrote about himself. I may still do that without trying, but it is not my intention.

Without knowing I was going to write anything, on November 1, 2018 I drove to the Lewis Grizzard Museum in his home town of

Moreland, Georgia. I phoned ahead to make sure it would be open on a Thursday, as some non-official website said it would be. I left a voice message to that effect, asking that they call me if they were in fact closed.

GPS guided me to the museum address, but it was not identified by any sign. It appeared to be a rustic brick building downtown, with little indication doors were unlocked. I was delighted to discover they were indeed open.

I use the term "they" loosely, as only one volunteer was there. Jimmy Haynes is a lifelong Moreland resident, having been away for a few years in the Air Force. (Thank you again for your service, Jimmy.) He was in school with Lewis, but a few years younger and did not claim to know him. Jimmy was informative to the extent his knowledge allowed. I

shared some Lewis details even
Jimmy did not know.

After a couple of hours I asked
Jimmy where the rest of Lewis's
"stuff" was. He advised that a lot
of it is at the University of
Georgia, but he did not know what
or where. I was heading to Athens
the following Monday, so I aspired
to press on there.

Earlier that week I went to the
UGA Grady College of Journalism
website to see if I knew any
alumni enrolled there at the same
time as Lewis. One name jumped out
at me. Betty Hudson was a charmer
at my fraternity when my older
brother was in school. She went on
to become a legend at National
Geographic, and she married
another National Geographic
legend, Boyd Matson. I have wanted
that guy's job since he began
hosting National Geographic
Explorer. I bug Betty occasionally

hoping her husband will call me with a voice message telling me to leave his wife alone. I apparently should bug her more often with greater vigilance, because Boyd has yet to call me.

Anyway, the day after my Moreland trek Betty replied to an email that she had met Lewis at UGA but did not know him. She referred me to another journalism legend, Dink NeSmith. Dink owns many community newspapers and lives in Athens. Fortunately he was in town and agreed to meet for coffee on short notice on November 7.

Dink advised that he tailgated near Lewis and was friendly with him, but would not claim that Lewis was his friend. We exchanged some colorful stories and agreed there is hardly a Lewis story that was not colorful. I asked Dink why it was that Lewis's legacy seems to be fading at UGA and elsewhere.

He replied, to paraphrase, "I guess someone just needs to champion the cause. Maybe that is you." I was floored.

My next stop was UGA's Hargrett Rare Book & Manuscript Library. There I hastily inspected 17 indexed document boxes and two half boxes. The document boxes contained original manuscripts, the half boxes a videotape and golf tournament trophy bag. I quickly concluded I would need to come back and spend several years in that inspection room.

On the way out I asked Hargrett librarians where Lewis's artifacts could be found. They referred me to Chantel Dunham, as had Dink NeSmith. Chantel is the foremost Lewis Grizzard expert on UGA staff. I contacted Chantel, and we agreed to meet on my next trip to Athens.

Dink also referred me to yet another legend, Jim Minter, former writer and editor of the Atlanta Journal and Constitution before and after the two papers merged. I began reading Jim, Jesse Outlar and Furman Bisher as a kid only shortly before I began reading Lewis. Dink observed that Jim was perhaps the only person who remained a constant in Lewis's life from his years at UGA until he died. I made a note to contact Mr. Minter as my head was filling and starting to spin.

About this time I took a look at the Georgia Writers Hall of Fame website, fully expecting to find Lewis there. He is absent. A guy by the name of Elias Boudinot is in there. I am sure he was a great writer, but I never heard of him or read his column. I pick on Elias only because he died in 1839 and is less likely to sue me than other inductees I never heard of.

To my knowledge Lewis never gambled on anything that affected the outcome of what he was working on. He took no performance enhancing drugs that allowed him to write better. Okay, that last statement is debatable, but there are no rules against legal substances being used to enhance one's writing.

Thus, I aspired to get Lewis into the Georgia Writers Hall of Fame by submitting an online nomination ballot. The template required that I fill in a response to this:

"Explain how this writer has made an enduring impact upon the study and understanding of Georgia, its people, history, and culture (2000 characters maximum):"

I felt like typing, "How about he is the most prolific and best loved stinking writer in Georgia history?" But that would be only 75 characters and a little snarky. This was the first time I nominated anyone for any hall of fame of any kind, so I was unsure how to go about it. I did not know who reads nomination ballot templates or what kind of mood they might be in. For all I knew Elias Boudinot might be one of the gatekeepers, and he might not like snarky. So I copied and pasted stuff from Lewis's obituary.

Little did I know that the Georgia Writers Hall of Fame induction ceremony was held in Athens on November 5. A UGA staffer had referenced it in emails hoping I would attend, but it was not the subject of my original inquiry and escaped my attention.

Little did I also know that Jim Minter and his wife had totaled a deer and their car in on their way to Athens for that induction ceremony. They were unscathed but shaken, as one would expect. Only after Chantel Dunham assured me they were okay and up to taking phone calls did I reach out to Mr. Minter. He agreed Lewis should be in the Hall of Fame, and we agreed to meet after Thanksgiving.

By this time I had accumulated a number of people to contact, along with email addresses and phone numbers. They included Loran Smith and other media giants, Sigma Pi fraternity brothers, golf and poker buddies, Newnan high school friends and Moreland childhood friends. My plate was filling, and this "investigation" was looking more and more like a book.

By completely separate coincidence I had real estate business in Athens. A guy wanted to buy a house there, and I needed an agent to help him. That agent was Barbara Dooley, and on November 11

I left her what had to be a
confusing voice message about real
estate and Lewis Grizzard. I then
called her Athens office and was
pleased to find her real estate
partner, Deanna, answering the
phone on a Sunday afternoon. As we
talked, Barbara returned my call.
Deanna said I should take it. I
told Deanna I would rather have a
voice message from Barbara Dooley.

Shortly thereafter Deanna Dooley,
not to be confused with Barbara's
real estate partner, emailed to
schedule a time for me to visit
with Vince and Barbara at their
Athens home. Deanna is their
eldest daughter and scheduling
manager, and a dang good one at
that. She proposed three dates,
and I jumped on the first one.
November 26, the Monday after
Thanksgiving. I was soon to be in
Hog Dawg Heaven.

That morning Deanna welcomed me at the door and showed me into the mother of all tasteful UGA man caves, the Dooley living room. Lewis once wrote that if you live a good life when you die you will go to Vince and Barbara's living room. He was correct. If Lewis was there I wish he would have tapped me on the shoulder at the very least.

I admired scores of Vince photos with Presidents, Prince Charles and others while trying not to hyperventilate. Barbara arrived first, and I did not know whether to plow ahead with questions or wait on Vince. I dove in with real estate questions, as they did not concern Vince. Only then did Barbara piece together that I was the guy who left the confusing voice message 2 weeks prior. She was in fact going to depart shortly to go meet the other

Deanna about the very real estate referral I sent to them.

Vince joined us, and I dove in with questions about Lewis's beloved dog Catfish and dozens of other topics. The Dooleys had as many questions for me as I had for them. They corroborated that I needed to speak with folks already on my schedule and offered several others. Barbara departed, leaving Vince and me alone. I got him to sign my copy of his epic, The Legion's Fighting Bulldog, for the 2nd time in a year. My sons will one day fight over that. But they will have to kill me first.

After 90 minutes Deanna entered and advised Vince he had five minutes before he needed to depart for Kirby Smart's SEC Championship press conference. Vince noted that, and we talked for another 15 minutes. We wrapped up, and I asked if I could attend that press

conference. He did not see why
not, and I could use my copy of
the book he had just signed as
credentials if anyone gave me a
hard time.

We departed separately, and I
proceeded to the campus parking
deck. My guess is Vince has a more
convenient space elsewhere, such
as wherever Vince wants to park in
the state of Georgia. When I got
to the deck the ticket dispenser
said "lot full", but a car pulled
in behind me. A grad assistant got
out and let me in with his badge.
I thought that was well and good,
but I got no ticket to get me out.
The grad assistant walked with me
to the press conference and gained
my admittance that would otherwise
require retina scans and DNA
samples that still would not have
gotten me in. He and I agreed to
chat after the press conference.

At the conference I sat next to Chuck Dowdle, kept my mouth shut and again tried to not hyperventilate. I introduced myself to Greg McGarity, Claude Felton, Jeff Schultz and other sports legends. I ate a box lunch to which I was not entitled next to Chip Towers while he wrote his press conference column. From each of these people I got recommendations for one to three more people to call. I then had to depart and complete an Atlanta writing job that interested me a whole lot less than sitting next to Chip Towers.

I met briefly with the grad assistant and thanked him again for getting me in. Then I asked how to get out. He gave me a parking deck pass that would be good even without a ticket in – or so he said. I dashed thru unfamiliar hallways past training facilities and people training I

never thought I would see up
close. Jake Fromm, Elijah
Holyfield, Isaac Nauta, Justin
Fields. I made it down to the
indoor practice facility thru
which I entered but went out the
wrong door.

Were he alive today Lewis would be
able to walk in and out of such a
UGA facility carte blanche, yet he
would have marveled at its
splendor just as I did. If I
succeed with this book maybe a
first edition will get me in along
with a press pass, a retina scan
and DNA samples.

Back to my attempt to leave. I
found myself on the outdoor
practice fields in cold wind and
with no apparent exit. The door
thru which I passed locked behind
me. Twenty minutes later I found
an open door back in and asked a
gathering at large how to get to
the parking deck. Jim Chaney asked

which parking deck. I replied that
I did not know because I had no
ticket. The main parking deck.
Coach Chaney, who himself has no
reason to be familiar with parking
decks, smirked and appointed
someone to guide me out. He would
not sit still for one more of the
12 selfies I scored that day. But
he did smile. Go Dawgs!!!

I got to the parking deck and
showed the pass that theoretically
was supposed to get me out free
without an entry ticket. That
caused minor confusion until I
showed the attendant my selfie
with Vince and Barbara and the
book Vince signed twice in one
year, including that morning.
Lesson learned: if one has no
proper credentials a volume of
confusing improper credentials
will often suffice. I got out in
time to complete the mundane
Atlanta writing project.

The following day I had coffee with Chantel Dunham at the main UGA library and gained a whole bunch of priceless new information. That lady better not retire like Vince and Barbara said she might before I complete this book. If she does I will have no choice but to ruin her retirement.

Days before I called my brother Scott in Wisconsin to update him on Grizzard stuff. He said I had to go to the Blue Willow Inn 35 miles south of Athens in Social Circle. I asked him what the Blue Willow Inn was and why did I have to go there. Scott and his wife once saw Lewis there, Lewis wrote about it as the epitome of great southern cooking and ate there all the time. So I scheduled a November 28 trip to Social Circle.

At the Blue Willow I met Patsy Joiner and Michael Cothren, the two managers. Louis and Billie Van

Dyke founded the restaurant in
1991. In 1992 it was about to go
out of business when Lewis
Grizzard showed up one November
night and wrote his article.
Louis, now deceased, met Lewis,
his widow Billie did not. But
Lewis put the place in 450
newspapers across the US, and the
place has been rocking ever since.

I ate the best home cooking on
earth, gained 10 pounds in one
sitting and scored a cookbook that
mentions Lewis. Now I must learn
to cook.

From Social Circle I continued
south in pursuit of Grizzard
cousins in Dublin. The Grizzards
on Lewis's dad's side are the
funny ones. The Words and
Atkinsons on his mom's side are
the nurturing ones. Lewis loved
both sides dearly, but there are
no Grizzards in Moreland.

I was told Everett, the blind piano repairman, is the Grizzard I need to talk to, but his sons Marshall or Skeeter might answer the phone. A lady answered the phone and fetched Everett. He was indeed hilarious.

Along the way I stopped at libraries large and small. Libraries are full of librarians and hopefully Lewis Grizzard books. Librarians know everything and almost everyone in town. I found one librarian who once cared for Catfish at the kennel where he boarded when Lewis traveled. At several libraries they want me to come back to talk about the book I'm writing. At very few libraries did I find more than one or two of Lewis's books. Again, I did not want to reread those books. I just want to know if they are there. With few exceptions they are not there, and that is sad.

Weeks ago I figured Lewis must have spent time at Lake Lanier, so I Googled "lewis grizzard lake lanier". To my astonishment and pleasant surprise the number one result is an article I wrote last year about a BBQ restaurant Lewis would have loved. Anyone reading this should go there. I since learned that Lewis was a Lake Oconee guy. More on his Lake Oconee roots shortly.

One of many contacts to whom Vince Dooley referred me is a favorite political hero, former Senator Saxby Chambliss. He and I spoke for 20 minutes on December 7. He shared a great story, one that is perhaps the most family friendly Lewis story to date.

Claude Felton has made the trains run on time at the UGA athletic Administration for decades. He referred me to his counterpart at Georgia Southern, Ric Mandes. Ric was instrumental in recruiting Erk Russell from UGA to reestablish football at Georgia Southern. Ric hosted Lewis often in Statesboro. He and I hope to meet soon.

Last week I spent three hours with yet another legend, Shelton Stevens. Shelton is a legend not only to UGA and Georgia but to thousands of children who are alive today because of his great deeds. He was Lewis's fraternity brother and attended Lewis's 4th and final wedding at Emory Hospital. I expected Shelton to share many stories I can publish. He indeed shared many, but I can only publish about 37% of them.

From there I went to meet Ernie Cain, Lewis's Ansley Country Club friend and Lake Oconee next door neighbor. Ernie was best man, or actually one of two best men, at Lewis's 4th and final wedding. With Ernie's permission I drove to

Lake Oconee for a walk around his house and Lewis's. Again, I need an Oconee real estate connection, so I had two reasons to head that way.

Ernie told me to call Jere Mills, likely the only Oconee real estate agent who would remember Lewis. Not only did Jere know Lewis well, he is now my go to guy for Oconee real estate.

Ernie also referred me to Carey Williams, the reason Lewis had a place on Oconee. Carey is owner of a legendary newspaper and the subject of a colorful Dink NeSmith story about Gene Talmadge's suspenders. I will meet with Jere Mills and Carey Williams once our schedules permit.

In the last two days I spoke with two of Lewis's Newnan High School teachers. One taught English, the other journalism. Both are very

well and retired in Moreland.
Lewis referenced great teachers
who had a profound influence on
his life and career. Richard Smith
and Sara Jane Skinner are two of
them. Sara's son Winston is News
Editor of the Newnan Time-Herald,
where Lewis published his first
articles as a grade school
student. With the help of Carol
Chancey of the Moreland Cultural
Arts Alliance, we will all meet
soon.

Yet to be scheduled are meetings
or phone calls with Jim Minter,
Loran Smith, Ray Goff, Herschel
Walker and many other notables as
distant as Nashville and Savannah.
Lewis Grizzard made lasting
friendships everywhere he went.
Virtually everyone I talk to is
enthusiastic about sharing their
Lewis stories. They then introduce
me to others who want to share
even more stories.

I do not intend to interview any ex-wife or even mention them by name. They each now lead private lives, and I wish them nothing but the best.

You may wonder why you should read this book after reading all this. Note that I have yet to share a single story. All I have done to this point is talk about the path I have taken to great people with the epic stories. I have collected those stories and will now commence tell them. The best is yet to come. Or so I hope.

Comments I Thought of After Writing the Introduction

I gave up trying to figure out the order of chapters in this book. Putting order into anything about Lewis is akin to getting ducks in a row when the ducks refuse to cooperate.

Do I put them in chronological order of Lewis's life? Chronological order as to when I talked to each person? Alphabetical order? How about complete disorder?

The chapters are in the order they are in, and you will just have to deal with it.

The first chapters I wrote pretty much conformed to the 500-800 words in a typical Lewis column. In later chapters I gave that up.

I just wrote until I ran out of
notes on a given subject. That
might mean I should go back and
add words to those early columns.
Yet if I do that this book may
never see light of day. Thus dear
contributors, if your chapter is
short please be flattered and
assume I wrote it early. If your
chapter is long please be
flattered and assume your story
was so fascinating I just could
not make it shorter. Either way,
please be flattered. I am
flattered in the extreme that you
gave me your time and attention.

There will be gaps. There will be
repetition. There will be confused
and inaccurate facts. Some
inaccuracies will be because I
can't nail the facts down. Others
will be because those who know the
facts can not seem to agree on
them. Yet other inaccuracies will
be because Lewis enjoyed
inaccuracy, as do his friends and

I. You can fact check every
chapter until you are blue in the
face and correct me if you dare.

Due to circumstances beyond my
control I have yet to speak with
many who I am told have
exceptional Lewis stories to tell.
Whether I speak with them for some
future addenda or another book
will depend on the success of this
book. If you want to see more
Lewis stories you can do your part
by mandating that every person you
know on earth buy this book. If a
single member of your staff
refuses to comply, fire them with
no severance package. Breaks some
rules if you have to.

As Larry Munson might say, I hope
you get the picture.

Chronology

October 20, 1946
Born, Fort Benning GA

1952
Parents separate, mother and Lewis
move to Moreland GA

1954
Mother Christine remarries

1956
Writes first articles for Newnan
Times-Herald

1965
Enrolls at University of Georgia,
writes for the Athens Daily News

1966
Marries first wife

1968
Hired as executive sports editor
by the Atlanta Journal

1969
Divorces first wife

1970
Father Lewis McDonald Grizzard,
Sr. dies

1975
Hired as executive sports editor
by the Chicago Sun-times

1976-77
Marries and divorces second wife

1977
Hired as sports columnist by the
Atlanta Constitution

1979
Transitions to humor columnist at
the Atlanta Constitution

1979
Publishes first book

1979
Marries third wife

1982
Divorces third wife

1980s & 90s
Began national stage performances.
Appeared on Tonight Show w/ Johnny
Carson, Letterman, Larry King
Live, Designing Women and more,
column syndicated to 450
newspapers

1982
First heart surgery

1984
Awarded journalism degree by
University of Georgia despite
being a few credits short

1985
Second heart surgery

1989
Mother Christine Word Grizzard
Atkinson dies

1993
Third heart surgery

1993
Publishes final book

1994
Marries fourth wife

1994
Fourth heart surgery

March 20, 1994
Died, Atlanta GA

Around the Circle

Whether at work, school or church, did you ever participate in the exercise where you get 5 or 10 people in a ring to tell the same short story?

It starts with folks gathering around standing or seated. By short story I mean a paragraph of two or three sentences. The first person reads the written paragraph and whispers it to the person next to them. By the time it gets to the last person the story or paragraph is entirely changed.

It would not be like that if you gathered a group of people like my son Kevin. He can still recite Billy Mays OxiClean infomercials verbatim that he has not heard in 10+ years. But I guarantee you will not gather a group of people like Kevin unless I give you a longer head start than I will allow for this column.

Writing a book about Lewis Grizzard is about like the

exercise described above, only more fun and with a lot more wrinkles.

First, Lewis died March 20, 1994, almost 25 years ago.

Second, people there may have sampled adult beverages.

Third, Lewis was never a stickler for the exact truth.

Take, for instance, what Lewis claimed to be the greatest headline in the history of sports journalism:

"DOGS TO PLAY C***S WITH D***S OUT"

Simply Google "greatest headline in the history of sports journalism" and you will find some 28 results, including a piece by yours truly at the top of page 3.

In the last two weeks I have spoken to several high profile people who knew Lewis well. No two accounts of the story are the same. At least two were in the room when the headline was written. One insists he wrote the headline, yet not verbatim as it appears above. I wholeheartedly believe that person. I think. At least he looked me square in the eye when he told me, and he did not choke on his coffee afterwards.

In the 28 some Google results you will find accounts that are just plain wrong. Whether the person who wrote the account embellished, Lewis embellished or the passage of time and/or adult beverages skewed the truth, the truth got skewed. I even have a message in to Happy Dicks, the subject of the headline. Why, I do not know. He had nothing to do with the story other than being "out" for the game in question.

I have scores of similar stories similarly skewed. And I have yet to meet with all participants who might serve to help me get the story straight. At best I might hope to agree upon a fraternity style quorum and arrive at some consensus that might approach the truth.

From his earliest days of writing for a newspaper, and we are talking grade school here, Lewis wrote with integrity. He even got himself fired from an unpaid writing job in high school by publishing an article with integrity instead of the version his faculty member approved.

The first person to hire Lewis at a big city newspaper (think larger than Athens GA) is a legendary journalist himself. He stated about Lewis in a December 10 email, "He was first and foremost, a SERIOUS journalist."

As a reporter, editor and newspaperman, in his early days Lewis was by all accounts an adherent to accuracy. It was only when he was unleashed to become a columnist did he begin to admittedly take liberties with facts. He was candid that he could write and say whatever he wanted, and it was when he began to do so that his career truly began to blossom.

Ironically, I lived happily in Chicago, the city that Lewis did not care for during Lewis's prime. Yes, I will say this repeatedly, as it is important to the context of … everything. Chicago papers did not run Lewis's by then syndicated columns, but I read his books and saw him on TV. The decline of Lewis's health, and even his death, completely escaped my notice.

So here I sit sorting through notes from in person and phone conversations with Lewis's remarkable friends. In some cases I have no notes, because they phoned me while I was driving – yes, legally using speakerphone or headset. But when certain people call you take that call, ask questions and listen. If you ask to call them back later when you have pen and paper handy you might not get that chance for months. And you dare not record a phone call with or without permission. I know there are apps that would allow me to do so. I want nothing to do with such an app.

In this book I will piece together what I can and hopefully come relatively close to the truth. I will do my utmost to tell only fun stories. If someone has a nasty comment I will not include it. This is about trying to write something as fun as what Lewis wrote.

At that I know I will fail. But I can try.

Meandering

One of many things I loved about Lewis was his tendency to meander when writing. A column or chapter would be on one topic, but he would squeeze in two or three side stories on the way to the main story.

This was before the internet or reading anything on the phone, so one had the pleasure of meandering along with Lewis. This was not a race to information. This was a relaxed ride full of enjoyable detours.

It is my nature too to meander when writing. I need to figure out new ways to say, "But I digress.".

However, as more people spend more time reading more stuff on smaller and smaller gadgets I have somewhat changed my writing style. Whereas I once wrote in long meandering sentences, properly punctuated to the best of my ability, I now write in shorter sentences.

More periods. Fewer commas. Shorter paragraphs too. As in the case of the last two blurbs, sometimes the result is not even a complete sentence. Lewis's favorite English teachers and mine would not approve, but they are now gone. Lewis wrote for his age, I write for mine.

I will attempt to refrain from too many quotes from Lewis's columns or books. That's what Lewis's columns or books and books are for. Hopefully those will one day become more readily available for purchase. Now you can find some via internet search, as I have done.

At times I will cite material from books and columns. I will attempt to do so only when I can not find that information from a primary source, like someone Lewis knew. I do not yet know how often that will be, because I have yet to meet with or even track down certain folks who knew Lewis.

One gap I must fill I have not yet been able to learn from a direct source. That is, what if any publication Lewis wrote for during his high school years?

In one of his books Lewis explained that in his freshman year of high school he covered his school's football games for the local paper. He needed his teacher's approval before submitting an article.

One week he wrote two articles. One was about his school's losing teams lousy coach. The other was an article he knew the teacher would approve. He submitted the

one he wanted about the lousy
coach. That ended Lewis's high
school writing career.

Another thing Lewis clarifies is
nothing is "career" related unless
someone is paying you to do
something. Thus, I may reference
early writing as the beginning of
his "career", when in fact no one
paid him to write the stuff being
discussed. I will strive to
minimize such confusion.

Jimmy Haynes

It was a dark and stormy night.

Well, not exactly, but it was a dank and overcast morning.

On November 1 I trekked to the Lewis Grizzard Museum in Moreland Georgia to see what was there.

It was reported to be open Thursdays thru Saturdays only, so I phoned to make sure I could get in. One never knows with small town attractions. I reached a voice message for a Carol Chancey to alert staff I was coming, along with a request to phone me if for whatever reason they might be closed. I did not hear back. They were indeed open. A good thing, as I traveled 80+ miles to get there, and I had no other business in Moreland for which I could expense mileage.

Upon arrival into town it was not so apparent if they were open - or even where they were. My GPS seemed to be undecided as to a couple of locations. The first one I chose was a large vintage building in the heart of 'downtown', yet the building was unmarked. Upon entering I was pleased to discover immediately familiar artifacts and a pleasant gentleman there to greet me.

Jimmy Haynes and I introduced ourselves, and I took in the scene. There was not very old Grizzard stuff, slightly older Erskine Caldwell stuff and considerably older general historic Moreland stuff. I mentioned to Jimmy that I had read Tobacco Road and other Erskine books in high school and did not remember them to be funny. I was there to see Lewis stuff. I was in the mood for funny on that dank and overcast day.

It's rather remarkable that two such famous authors came out of a town as small as Moreland. The 2010 census showed a population of 399. Were Lewis alive he would likely write something to the effect of 'Mayor Delvin Swanson moved from his cabin to his shed just outside the town line during the week the census was taken so Moreland would be small enough to make the Federal Government spring for 70% of the new seven foot extension to the hosiery mill mailroom.'

Among the first things I did was ask Jimmy to take the obligatory photo of me with Lewis and Catfish.

I kinda wish Lewis was a 3D cut
out so I could swing my arm around
him best buddy style.

As it is that picture looks a bit
awkward. I'm pretty sure Lewis
would agree.

There were many cool Lewis
possessions on display, including
this quilt Lewis's Mama made out
his jammies, shown with the book
he wrote about her.

I got to talking to Jimmy about
Lewis, asking a ton of questions,
one of which was, did Jimmy know
him. Jimmy said he was born in
Moreland and lived there his
entire life with the exception of
years in the Air Force. He said he
was a couple of years younger than

Lewis, had certainly met him but could not really say he knew him.

That is unusual modesty. When people ask if I knew a celebrity from where I grew up I claim to have been their very closest friend, particularly if they are no longer around to declare me a liar. If the celebrity was female I won't even dare confess here how close I claim to have been with that female. But Jimmy was modest.

Jimmy told me stories about the many artifacts on display. I told him a few factoids he did not know but I remembered from long ago. We visited for two hours. I was the only customer that day, and that troubled me. Jimmy offered to drive me to Lewis's grave, then he directed me to Lewis's childhood home. He said he thought the home may be in foreclosure, and that troubled me as well.

Back to the reason my GPS was
confused earlier in the day. The
first Lewis Grizzard Museum was
located in a different building
owned and operated by Lewis's
close childhood friend, Dudley
Stamps. Dudley graciously agreed
to donate all of his stuff to the
new larger facility with more and
better display space.

To the side in the new museum are
many plastic bins of Lewis
artifacts not yet indexed or even
inventoried. Jimmy let me poke
through one or two bins. It felt

like handling Holy Grail stuff but did not say so lest Jimmy think I was even creepier than he already thought.

Before we parted I asked Jimmy where the rest of Lewis's 'stuff' was. He thought UGA had a lot of stuff but he did not know what or where. Fortunately I was destined for Athens the following Tuesday.

Postscript:

Since drafting this chapter I discovered Jimmy Haynes was holding back on me. Maybe it is because I only met him that day. Maybe it is because he is just a holding back kind of guy. Whatever, he was holding back.

In a December 7 issue of The Newnan Times-Herald, Jimmy wrote of greatness. This is the very periodical that first published Lewis Grizzard work, and Jimmy wrote on the same subjects that Lewis covered in his first article, Namely:

1. Lewis Grizzard greatness.
2. Little League baseball.

There was a notable difference between Lewis's first 1956 article and Jimmy's 2018 article.

Lewis wrote about his own little league team, and the headline was that at age 10 Lewis pitched a no-hitter.

Jimmy wrote about his own little league team, yet he wrote his article when he was well beyond age 10. And in Jimmy's article, Jimmy broke up a Lewis Grizzard no-hitter in the dramatic last at bat of the game.

Jimmy stated that as a youth he was a triple threat. He couldn't hit, run fast or field a grounder.

I am beginning to like Jimmy even more than the day I met him. This is a far cry from Lewis's youthful self-aggrandizement. Yet I like Lewis for his youthful self-aggrandizement. Writing is kinda funny that way.

Candidly, I like Jimmy's and Lewis's stuff better than Erskine Caldwell's depressing stuff, but I digress. Plus, it is shabby form to dis a writer who is no longer around to defend himself. But if Erskine was around, my guess is his self defense would be depressing.

Barbara and Vince Dooley

Lewis wrote that if you live a good life when you die you will go to Vince and Barbara Dooley's living room.

That is where I found myself at 10 AM on Monday, November 26, 2018. I was alone and had to check my pulse. To my knowledge I was still alive.

I found it remarkable that the first UGA legend after Dink NeSmith who would invite me to talk was in my mind the greatest of them all, Vince. Vince did not invite me per se. Deanna Dooley, his capable and charming daughter and social secretary, invited me. The week prior she suggested three days and times. Once I stopped hyperventilating I jumped on the first open slot, Monday morning after Thanksgiving.

Knowing the Dooleys are award winning gardeners, I prefaced to Deanna that we could save time by skipping any tour they may offer of their garden. This would be in everyone's best interest, as when I even look at a plant it begins to wilt. Deanna took note. Neither of us wanted that morning to be the beginning of the end of Dooley gardening awards.

Deanna greeted me at the door, guided me to the living room and advised her parents would join me shortly. For a few minutes I took in sheer magnificence. UGA Dawgs Memorabilia Heaven combined with freshly placed Christmas decor. Bulldog Man Cave on Steroids balanced by a touch of Tasteful Goddess Holiday Ornamentation.

Barbara was the first to enter. After introductions I asked if we should wait for Vince or just dive in. We dove in. I think I began with a story about trick or treating for charity at their house circa 1977 dressed as a nurse. I was so pretty that night Vince might have asked me out were he not a devoted husband and had Barbara not been standing by his side.

Barbara and I then talked about general Lewis stuff and what I was doing. At that early date I was not yet sure what I was doing. Being the goddess she is, Barbara put me at ease.

Vince soon joined us, so I exhibited shabby form by starting over and just talking faster. No telling how long they might indulge me before Deanna showed me the door.

Once I perceived Vince and Barbara were similarly up to speed I cut to the chase. "What is heaven's name gave you the idea that Lewis Grizzard was responsible enough to take care of a puppy?!"

I did not ask it in such a snarky fashion. To catch readers up, the Dooley's gave Catfish to Lewis. I was curious how that happened. So I asked, somewhat more politely than written above, but with the same angle.

Barbara replied, to paraphrase, "We did not give Catfish to Lewis. Lewis took him."

I asked her to elaborate. She and Vince elaborated. If I continue to write in dialogue form this chapter will become a whole new book, so I will return to narrative.

Vince and Barbara owned two champion bloodline Labrador Retrievers, Herschel Walker and Miss Dixie. I will let you figure out the male and female part. The pair produced some champion bloodline litters, but Catfish was not from one of those litters.

It seems Miss Dixie could not fully satiate Herschel's romantic interests, and he fathered a number of litters around the Dooley neighborhood. Apparently 1980s Athens leash laws are not what they are today. Or maybe anyone named Dooley is exempt from Athens leash laws. They should be.

Here I will introduce creative license by depicting a scene as I envision it, not as the Dooleys described it.

One day circa 1983 Herschel was in the mood for love. Miss Dixie may not have been in the mood, or maybe she had a chunk of Science Diet stuck between her teeth. For whatever reason Herschel sought romance elsewhere.

On the prowl Herschel caught the scent of a female in heat. Soon he caught an eye full of that female. A lovely lass indeed. After an appropriate period of canine courtship and perhaps some discussion of pre-nuptial issues the two hooked up. Perhaps they enjoyed a celebratory smoke afterwards. Some 60 days later a glorious litter of ½ Herschel offspring came into the world.

The household where that lass resided happened to be good friends of the Dooleys. Rather than engaging in some shotgun wedding or feud that might last for decades, the neighbors celebrated. The Dooleys took the litter and set out to find homes for the handsome pups.

Barbara adorned each critter with a Georgia red ribbon and bow. She and Vince set off with the adorable varmints to some UGA function, where they paraded them briefly in a wagon. They then cut the puppies loose so they could demonstrate their puppy cuteness.

Then Lewis Grizzard showed up, fresh from a broken romance. He eyeballed the pups and declared, "I need me something loyal. I need me a dog. I want that one."

The Dooleys had intended for one of their kids to take the whelp Lewis selected, yet they recognized Lewis's urgent and desperate need. Their child's loss was Lewis's gain. Lewis wrote the rest. On the drive home he blurted out "Catfish! That's what I'll call you!". Catfish awoke from his cozy back seat blanket, perked up and proceeded to soil the entire back seat.

The rest is history. Catfish went on to become almost as famous and popular as Lewis. After comedy performances in places like Seattle people would say to Lewis, "You were pretty funny and all, but did you bring Catfish and when can I see him?"

But that is not the entire history, and that is not the entirely correct history. You will read the entire correct history here first.

You see, the female pooch by which Herschel sired Catfish's litter was not a champion bloodline Labrador Retriever. Not even close. She was a seductive redhead. She was a - gasp - champion bloodline Irish Setter.

Though the offspring were pure black and by all appearances were Labs, the Dooleys realized they had to come up with another pedigree - and quick. They dubbed the progeny a proud new, one time only breed: Irish Walkers.

When they announced this I howled. The world had been hoodwinked, with Lewis and the Dooleys doing the hoodwinking. The Dooleys never aspired to keep anything a secret. It's just that the details somehow got lost over the decades.

It took 48 hours for the genius of "Irish Walkers" to occur to me. I was thinking, "did they not run as fast as Labs or setters?"

Two days later it struck me. Irish as in Irish Setter. Walker as in Herschel Walker. Doh!

In this era of diversity it is ironic and somehow fitting to discover that Catfish was of mixed lineage. In fact, a half-breed. Lewis might observe that would facilitate easier acceptance as an Ivy League law school professor, but I shall not attempt that here.

A key detail I neglected. When Vince joined Barbara and me that AM, I said I last saw him at a December 2017 East Cobb Kroger book signing. I was with Kevin and Ben, my teenage sons, and he autographed his Civil War masterpiece, The Legion's Fighting Bulldog. I brought out the book and handed it to Vince along with a sharpie.

"You want me to sign it again?!"

"You bet your sweet ass I do Coach." Except I answered more politely. Kevin, Ben and I now possess the world's one and only copy of a Vince Dooley epic signed by the author twice within a twelve month period. Once in a Marietta grocery store, once in the author's remarkably tasteful man cave living room. When one owns a priceless collectible it is vital to document provenance. Kevin, Ben and I will never part with the volume, but if we did bidding would start at 1.43 billion dollars.

I asked the Dooleys about Cornbread, Lewis's supposedly too wild Lab that crashed through closed windows with excitement every time Lewis pulled into the driveway. Lewis apparently found a good new home for Cornbread. But the Dooleys knew nothing about any second Lab. Cornbread must have come from elsewhere.

I veered off Lewis to express that I was in Chicago when rumors circulated that Vince might go to Auburn and Pat Dye might come to UGA, each returning to coach at their alma maters. I could get almost zero SEC news in Chicago, and the thought nauseated me. I expect it nauseated Lewis too, but I have yet to find what he wrote on the subject. Barbara commented, "Yes, we came close to moving." I gushed, thanking them and God for not letting it happen.

Barbara had to depart for an appointment. I wanted badly to kiss her on the lips but exercised restraint and settled for a hug. I may have embellished that. It might have only been a firm and gracious handshake.

That left me one on one, mano on mano, with Vince.

I recalled to Vince that Lewis wrote he and Vince arrived at UGA the same year. Lewis got a room at Reed Hall and a typewriter. Vince got a house and a car. But Vince had it tougher. He had to turn around the UGA football program. And turn it around Vince did.

I asked Vince if he remembered the first time he met Lewis. Vince was not certain, but it was before this classic 1966 photo:

COACH VINCE DOOLEY AND REMINDER OF GREAT WIN
Daily News Sports Editor Lewis Grizzard Makes Presentation

The headline reads, "Oh, Hot Diggity Dog, Mr. Dooley, You Have Wrecked Ole Tech Again!"

That looks like something I might have written as editor of my 1970 grade school High Point Hotline. But if it was good enough for Vince and Lewis it is more than good enough for me.

Lewis and the Dooleys obviously became lasting friends. Vince talked about colorful experiences later shared by others I had yet to meet. Others shared so much color on some of those experiences I can not print them in a family friendly publication. None involve off color behavior by the Dooleys. They involve off color behavior often in the presence of the Dooleys. More on those in other chapters.

Vince and I discussed publishers, Lewis's, Vince's and whoever my publisher might be. Vince offered sage publishing advice. I will not go into that here, as it will not likely interest anyone without anything to publish. Plus I do not wish to alienate any enterprise that may be a candidate to publish this or anything else I write.

The ever gracious Deanna entered to announce, "Dad, you've got five minutes." To which Vince asked, "Five minutes for what?" "Before you have to depart for the Kirby Smart press conference."

Vince rolled his eyes and said something to the effect of, "They want me to come to those things but never ask me to say anything." I groveled and asked if I could attend, and if so, with what credentials. He suggested that my copy of his book autographed moments ago combined with the selfies on my phone might suffice if anyone asked. That was all the permission I needed.

Fifteen minutes after Deanna's five minute warning Vince and I were still asking and answering each other's questions. I read somewhere that it is unwise to press one's luck with even the most gracious of hosts. I suggested that we each depart for a press conference where one of us

would be conspicuous by his
absence and the other would be
conspicuous by his unauthorized
presence. We struck a deal. I said
if anyone got cross with Vince for
being late to blame Peter
Stoddard. Not sure if he needed
that excuse.

As I exited we paused for one last
selfie. It unfortunately does not
reveal the majesty of multicolored
Japanese maples spanning across
the Dooley front acreage. I only
hope they did not wilt before I
was off the property for at least
a week or two.

Claude Felton, Ric Mandes & BA Anderson

The day I crashed Kirby Smart's pre SEC Championship game press conference with the false credentials of Vince Dooley's twice autographed book, a selfie taken with Vince less than 17 minutes earlier and my 1976 UGA student ID placed in an official looking lanyard I ran into other famous guys.

The first was Claude Felton, who I first met in 1976 by way of introduction from Myers Hall freshman roommate Pete Matey. Pete was a UGA pommel horse specialist on the gym team before Title 9 killed UGA men's gymnastics. Claude was the guy who made UGA Athletics Administration trains run on time. He still is.

Claude stonewalled and claimed he had few Lewis stories to share. I interrogated him again weeks later when I found him issuing bulletins outside Athens First United Methodist Church. At least Claude is devout and consistent when he stonewalls.

Claude said I needed to talk to Ric Mandes in Statesboro. I asked why, but Claude was kinda busy making sure the Kirby Smart press conference train run on time. He told me he would email me Ric's contact info, and I would find out why Ric was a good guy to talk to when I reached him. Ya right.

Well, I beat Mr. Smarty Pants Claude to the punch by finding Ric Mandes before Claude could send me his contact info. I first found something Ric wrote that led me to believe he was with the Statesboro Herald. Then I saw he wrote what he wrote as a guest columnist.

I then suspected Ric was some official at Georgia Southern University, the esteemed institution where my brother Scott matriculated when no one was watching. I was almost right. Ric is a retired esteemed official at Georgia Southern University.

Ric is a retired Georgia Southern official who once pissed off a

whole lot of UGA people, myself
included. Ric was largely
responsible for luring Erk Russell
from Athens to establish the
Georgia Southern football program
before they had a single football.
Ric is the guy who had to rush out
and buy a football before Erk
arrived to demonstrate the college
was serious about football. That
must have been one fine football
because Erk took the job and
stayed quite a while.

I do not recall exactly how Ric
met Lewis, but Erk may have had
something to do with it. Lewis may
have concluded that if Statesboro
was good enough for Erk maybe
Lewis should check it out.
Actually, now that I type this I
recall Lewis met Ric before Erk
arrived since Ric himself was well
traveled and ran in the same
sports honcho circles as Lewis.

Lewis took to Statesboro, and he took to Ric. He also took to Erk, who became a frequent tennis partner. Lewis, Erk and Ric also became frequent gambling partners and consumers of adult beverages.

Ric co-authored <u>Erk: Football, Fans & Friends</u>, Erk's 1991 autobiography. Yet another book I gotta read when I am done writing this one. At UGA and GSU Erk was a football legend. Among many Erkisms that survive and thrive today is GATA - get after their ass. UGA legend Bobby Poss attributes that to Lewis - see his chapter. But it was Erk who invented it. Today folks hijack the acronym simply due to universal popularity, as follows:

Georgia Academic Team Association

Groundstaff Aviation Technics and Administration

Greek American Translators Association

Girls Aiming Toward Achievement

Those are all a crock. Were it not for Erk people would come up with more sensible names for the above groups of hooligans. I only hope they do not buy this book and sue me. Buy the book yes, sue me no.

Ric hosted Lewis at his home, sometimes for weeks on end. Lewis sometimes needed quiet from the storm or a quiet place to convalesce before or after a medical procedure. The 1981 photo above is Lewis at the Statesboro Holiday Inn. Lewis called Ric on short notice to ask if he could come visit for Christmas, Lewis otherwise having no one with whom to spend it. Ric said of course Lewis was welcome, but there was no room at the Mandes Inn. Family was in town.

Lewis developed a lasting love for Statesboro. When his cardiologist said he could travel following a surgery Lewis called Ric and said, "Ric I want to come to Statesboro, ride into the countryside and look at God's Southern homes with hound dogs asleep under the porch."

Ric and Lewis had another cohort by the name of Billy Anderson, better known as BA. BA began in Statesboro but ended up in Athens, largely due to friendship with Lewis. Ric chose to settle down, reduce and eventually eliminate his consumption of adult beverages.

BA was not yet ready to settle down, nor was Lewis.

I phoned BA and got a few remarkable stories, only one of which can I share. BA and Lewis caroused between marriages. BA phoned Lewis to tell him BA was engaged - again. Lewis halfheartedly wished BA well, likely saddened that he might lose a carousing buddy.

Soon thereafter Lewis called BA with an announcement, good news and bad news:

"Good news is I am buying your honeymoon to Hawaii."

"Bad news is I am coming with you."

At the Atlanta airport BA introduced his fiancée to Lewis and his date. They compared notes on things they had in common, including their marriages and divorces. Between the four of them they had a total of 10 divorces. Lewis's date accounted for 5 or 6.

They had a grand time in Hawaii and returned without any incident I can publish. A few days later Lewis called BA to announce strictly bad news. He called that Hawaii date to ask her out. She was engaged - again.

The epic question is whether that woman's new fiancée was aware that the woman of his future had just spent a week in Hawaii with Lewis Grizzard. There are some questions that have no ready answers.

Claude Felton, see what you started?

Blue Willow Inn

I am blessed with perhaps the most
fun project in the world, writing
about the most fun writer of my
lifetime. Lewis blessed so many in
ways he never knew. None more than
Social Circle's Blue Willow Inn.

From Athens I called my brother
Scott in Madison Wisconsin to
catch him up on my Lewis research.
Scott commented, "You are so close
you ought to go to the Blue Willow
Inn."

I asked Scott what that was and
why should I go there.

He replied, "It is a restaurant in
Social Circle Lewis saved from
going out of business and ate at a
lot."

Scott and his late wife Patty - a
saint if there ever was one -
lived in Covington and Conyers

early in their marriage. Six years younger than Scott, I was single and palled around with them a lot either stag or with a girlfriend in tow.

Do not ask about when Patty's horse Misty tried to decapitate me by galloping full speed under a tree limb barely higher than Misty was tall. I somehow avoided decapitation and remained in the saddle. But it was not pretty, and I am pretty sure I whimpered afterward in front of my girlfriend.

On days when none of their horses were trying to decapitate me Patty, Scott and I went for drives to nearby old towns to stroll sidewalks and poke around antique stores. Social Circle was one of those towns.

Years after I moved to Chicago Scott and Patty dined at the Blue

Willow and saw Lewis there one day. Next day they were thrilled to see Lewis wrote about that visit.

Given that context, Scott's suggestion astonished me. I was heading south from Athens in a couple of days and would pass through Social Circle. I phoned the Blue Willow Inn and announced I would like to drop in and talk to anyone who remembered Lewis Grizzard. They gave me the name of manager Patsy Joiner who was too busy at the moment to come to the phone. She would expect me.

Upon arrival Patsy informed me she
never met Lewis, nor had any
current Blue Willow staff. The
only person who ever met him was
the late founder Louis Van Dyke.

Co manager and chef Michael
Cothren soon joined the
conversation while Patsy leisurely
worked on a bowl of soup and I
wolfed food down and dashed back
for 3rd and 4th helpings of
everything.

Patsy and Michael explained Blue
Willow history. Before it was a
restaurant Gone With the Wind
author Margaret Mitchell often
visited owners of the then private
home.

In 1991 the Van Dyke family bought
the building and undertook
extensive restoration before
opening a restaurant. In their
second year of business the Blue
Willow was struggling. In March

1992 Lewis had business in Social Circle and asked where he could find a restaurant serving Southern home cooking. His associate recommended the Blue Willow, changing world history. Literally.

Lewis wrote a column about the restaurant's exceptional home cooked everything, including fried green tomatoes.

The column ran in 280+ papers across the country and put Blue Willow on everyone's bucket list before the term bucket list even existed.

Estonian athletes flocked to the place during the 1996 Summer Olympics in Atlanta. No one at the Blue Willow remembers them or knows why wintery Estonia would send athletes to any Summer Olympics. That is not the point.

Clint Eastwood, Helmut Kohl, Helen
Mirren and other celebs have dined
at the Blue Willow. They make it a
practice to give famous folks
their privacy and not name names.
They gave me consent to name those
names.

Lewis dined there only the one
time. He soon became too ill to
travel. He died 2 years after his
only visit.

They named a room after Lewis, and
the exceptional everything they
served in 1992 is just as
exceptional 25 years later.

Both Patsy and Michael were thoroughly familiar with Lewis's writing and Catfish, depicted in the photo above. They were among the first with whom I shared the Catfish Pedigree Scandal discovered only days earlier. They were aghast. See the Barbara and Vince Dooley chapter.

I thanked Patsy and Michael profusely and left stuffed with a copy of the hefty Blue Willow Inn Cookbook. Somewhere in there is mentions Lewis Grizzard. If I knew how to cook and/or read cookbooks maybe I could find whatever it says about him.

When I called brother Scott to report all this he was stunned to learn he and Patty were there on the day of Lewis's only visit. I was equally stunned that I discovered the Blue Willow only by way of a timely phone to Madison

Wisconsin. I need to call Scott more often if he's gonna turn me on to such cool places.

Things got stranger from there.

That afternoon I drove to Macon and stopped at the Monroe library to use WiFi and see if they had any out of print Lewis books. I asked at the desk if anyone had heard of Lewis. A lady perked up and said, "Sure. I used to take care of Catfish."

I was floored. Catfish died 25 years ago.

She was a vet tech who called on the Loganville kennel where Catfish lodged while Lewis traveled. I asked the lady if Catfish was the perhaps the best looking Labrador Retriever she had ever seen. She said he was in fact a magnificent Labrador Retriever specimen.

Then I dropped the Catfish
Pedigree Scandal on her. She was
aghast. See the Barbara and Vince
Dooley chapter. Good thing the
lady is a capable librarian. She
may lose her veterinarian
technician credentials.

Early Influences

Lewis Grizzard was pleased to share credit where credit was due to people who guided him on his path to journalism. In one of his books he talked about two high school teachers he worked hard to impress, H. Richard Smith and Sarah Jane Skinner.

I was thrilled to discover that both still live in Moreland. Not only did they impress Lewis, he impressed them.

My path to Richard and Sara was indirect, as all things about Lewis seem to be. I first discovered that a legendary Newnan High English teacher who once taught both Lewis and country music star Alan Jackson is still teaching at the school. Barbara Landreth began when JFK was president and is one of the longest serving teachers in the

state of Georgia. When I reached
Barbara she informed me she only
had Lewis for homeroom. She
advised I needed to talk to
Richard and Sara. Remarkable.

My first conversation was with
Richard. He advised that Lewis was
enrolled in Newnan's college bound
prep curriculum, the most
ambitious program offered. Richard
taught straight English, and he
immediately recognized Lewis to be
a special talent. Not only was
Lewis well disciplined, he was an
enthusiastic learner and often
asked for additional assignments.
Richard was more than happy to
oblige.

Lewis credited Richard with
teaching him the love of words. He
declared the man to be a walking
dictionary.

Richard would bait Lewis with
themes such as, compare a tomato

to a redhead, or the more tame, compare a tomato to an onion. Richard unfortunately does not remember or have copies of what Lewis produced as a result. He simply remembers that if he gave Lewis the ball, he would run with it.

Lewis's comic instincts emerge early as well. As in the little boy who had a pet dinosaur named Thesaurus. Richard always advocated the use of a thesaurus vs a dictionary. Lewis obviously learned early on how to suck up to teachers when he needed to as well.

Richard recalls that Lewis had a rare mastery of language, exercising brilliant use of adjectives and adverbs unlike many accomplished authors. Richard told Lewis it was perfectly okay to use sentence fragments for emphasis when textbooks of the day would not allow such liberties. Lewis would often ask Richard to stay late for additional time to brush up on diction and polish his style. Richard knew him for crisp, fresh staccato cadence that belied his education level.

Richard began his career when the principal called to say he needed a summer school English teacher. He jumped at the opportunity and stayed on for decades. Richard sums up his teaching philosophy as follows:

"If you fail to educate both the mind and soul, you have failed to educate the student."

Sara Jane Skinner taught English too, but in Lewis's case she taught journalism. Sara negotiated with the Newnan Times-Herald newspaper would permit Newnan High School students to submit a weekly 'Tiger Tracks' section covering high school sports and other activities. The only condition was that students had to take a journalism class that did not yet exist. To create a journalism class Sara purchased the best journalism textbook she could find. She read one chapter ahead the night before each class and launched the first Newnan High journalism curriculum to an enthusiastic hoard of 25 to 30 students.

Lewis and others called Sara Gypsy Woman due to her dark good looks and fondness for purple garments. Lewis once mused that the two most attractive teachers at Newnan High were Sara and a lady who taught algebra. Lewis favored Sara, as he could not envision any algebra teacher maintaining her beauty for long. Here again we see Lewis's propensity to suck up to teachers. All except algebra teachers.

Lewis's mother Christine was an admired first grade teacher in Moreland, and Sara knew her and her extended Word family. She tried not to take special interest in Lewis, but it was only natural to see what your friends' kin can do when he makes it to your class. Lewis excelled until he didn't. Or did.

Back to the Tiger Tracks section. Another condition of Newnan High students writing for the Newnan Times-Herald was that faculty had to approve everything submitted for publication. Faculty, as in Sara. One week Sara approved one piece, but Lewis submitted another. The result was considerable uproar, as the published piece approved by precocious Lewis alone was critical of Newnan High's losing football coach. This ended Lewis's contributions to the Newnan Times-

Herald for the duration of his high school years.

The last time Sara saw Lewis was at Newnan's beloved but now sadly closed Scott's book store. She stood in line to get Lewis to sign his last book. As she reached his desk he stopped everything, got up, gave her a big hug and pulled up another chair so she could sit next to him. He told her he planned to come back to sit with her on her front porch, chat and he would spit tobacco. This is the first reference I have heard about Lewis chewing or spitting, and I expect it was a rhetorical comment. Lewis died before he could return to Sara's porch and spit.

The caveat to all this is years ago H. Richard Smith was at either the high school or a library in a book storage room. He looked down and saw an old journalism textbook

on the floor. When he opened it he
saw Lewis Grizzard inscribed as
the last apparent owner. Richard
either paid a paltry amount or was
invited to take it. He still owns
it. I have yet to see it but will
soon.

Remarkable.

Jim Minter

Jim Minter may be the first newspaper writer I read.

In about 5th grade I graduated from comics to the sports page, and that is where I found Jim, along with Jesse Outlar, Furman Bisher and eventually Lewis Grizzard. This was in the Atlanta Journal and Constitution, once competing afternoon and morning papers, then semi-merged, now entirely merged. I will not split hairs here about which I read when.

At some point Jim Minter became less visible as a writer. That is because he got promoted to editor. He still wrote columns, only less often. He was one of my early heroes. Some say he was Lewis's primary hero.

Dink NeSmith suggested I talk to Jim and made proper introductions. He observed that Jim was probably Lewis's closest friend for the longest span of Lewis's life. I will speculate that Jim was also a stabilizing influence on a guy whose life resisted stabilization.

Dink cautioned that only days before he and I met, Jim and his wife Anne totaled both a Lexus and a deer on their way to Athens for the annual Georgia Writers Hall of Fame induction ceremony. Both Jim and Anne emerged unscathed but shaken. The big buck fared far less well, as did the Lexus.

When I reached Jim by phone I felt him out hoping for assurance that he and Anne were okay. They were, though Jim confessed that at age 87 it takes longer to recover from high speed collisions and deployed airbags than it should. I experienced something similar at almost exactly half his age, so I empathized. We agreed to meet after Thanksgiving but talk and correspond in the interim as the need and schedules permitted.

Given the busy holidays, a totaled car, convalescence and the fact that my hero is 87 I did not want to wear out Jim's invitation to communicate. I sent him emails for context on my progress, advising that what began as research may be evolving into a book. I expressed my surprise and chagrin that Lewis is not a member of the Georgia Writers Hall of Fame, the very group at whose ceremony Jim would have appeared had it not been for a pesky and unfortunately deceased deer. I informed Jim that I had nominated Lewis for that Hall of Fame by way of a UGA website template.

When I dared to call after giving Jim time to mend he was both gracious and enthusiastic on the phone. He opined that Lewis was possibly excluded from the Hall of Fame due to deceased member Pat Conroy's animosity toward Lewis. That stymied me and led to later research. Jim observed that the prolific Furman Bisher was inducted into the Hall only weeks ago. Judges apparently did not deem sports writing to be writing.

I indeed researched Pat Conroy and Lewis. You can Google it for yourself. Conroy once wrote something to the effect of Lewis representing everything that is wrong with the South. Lewis replied that he liked Conroy's

work and was sorry Conroy felt
that way. In other words, Lewis
turned the other cheek, something
Lewis rarely did. I read most of
Conroy's work. It is full of angst
that makes you want to cry.
Lewis's work is full of angst that
makes you most often laugh and
only occasionally cry. I prefer
laughter to crying.

Leading up to our meeting I
informed Jim that no matter what
he insisted I would address him as
"Mr. Minter". This was in honor of
him being the only person Lewis
addressed as "mister" his entire
life. Mr. Minter asked what the
heck I was talking about. I told
him I had read it somewhere and
would find it. Thereafter we
bantered back and forth as Jim
a/k/a Mr. Minter and Peter a/k/a
Mr. Stoddard. I have never had so
much fun bantering with a hero in
my life. Until I had lunch with
that hero.

I met Jim for lunch at 11:30 December 18 at a Fayetteville GA spot he recommended near his home.

I first caught him up on stuff I thought I had learned. He graciously listened, only occasionally interrupting with minor corrections of fact. I told him about Lewis being turned away from the Atlanta Journal reception desk as a high school senior. He showed up to announce he would have a UGA journalism degree in four years and wanted to talk to someone about working for the paper as a student. After he was rebuffed he snuck up for a peek into Furman Bisher's vacant office and told himself he would return in four years. Ironically, it was Jim a/k/a Mr. Minter who invited Lewis back, and he invited him in less than four years.

I will now dispense with Jim a/k/a
Mr. Minter at Mr. Minter's, I mean
Jim's, insistence. I will go ahead
and say that a Coweta County
Visitors Bureau website is the
source of confusion. They no doubt
got erroneous info in good faith
and went with it. It is the
continuing nature of Lewis's life
and legend. I later found that
source again and brought it to
Jim's attention. If he wishes to
correct his home county visitors
bureau that is up to him.

Jim found Lewis via a trip to UGA,
his own alma mater. He needed a
sports guy and wanted to get
opinions of people he knew in
search of a candidate. He spoke to
the likes of Joel Eaves, Dan
McGill and Vince Dooley. They each
directed Jim to one guy, Lewis
Grizzard. Only one senior UGA
athletic person specifically
advised against hiring Lewis. That
cemented it. Jim did not like that

person. If that person did not like Lewis, Lewis had to be the perfect choice.

When Jim approached him Lewis was a couple of courses short of graduation. Jim offered a job only under the condition that Lewis complete his degree, sooner rather than later. Lewis earnestly consented. If on schedule Lewis would have collected his diploma in 1968. I have seen it written that Lewis eventually took correspondence courses. Erroneous news again. Per Jim, in 1984 UGA just gave Lewis his journalism degree.

Jim first met Lewis at a UGA baseball game. One noteworthy memory from that day is Lewis had used a press box funnel and garden hose arrangement so he could pee from his seat without missing any of the game. Invention of the device is loosely credited to Dan

Magill, and it was used by many "on demand". One of many roles Magill filled at UGA was baseball scorer. Occasionally a player's girlfriend got an eyeful she did not expect when peering into the press box to inquire if Magill scored her beau's last play as a hit or error. Served her right for intruding on the scorekeeper.

In 1968 Jim hired Lewis as reporter, soon promoted to executive sports editor. He edited very ably for years, and this is where dates and years get fuzzy. I show Lewis as taking the same job at the Chicago Sun-Times from 1975 to 1977, but this would have Lewis editing uninterrupted at the Journal for 7 years. That seems too long for Lewis to have sat still in an editor's desk. Even Wikipedia is no help with dates.

To quote from Furman Bisher's March 21, 1994 column eulogizing

Lewis, this may partially explain the sequence of events:

"Jim Minter had left The Journal to become managing editor of The Constitution, and we needed an executive sports editor to replace him. After a week of agonizing, I gave the job to Grizzard. I couldn't have done him a worse disservice. It was sort of like hitching Whirlaway to a plow."

"It was Minter who unscrambled his career for him. It was Minter who discovered the writer in him, first as a sports columnist in The Constitution. It was soon obvious that was like putting him in hobbles, restricted his humor and his breadth of subjects. When Minter moved him to the general section of the paper, it was like a liftoff. Grizzard was in orbit."

Concise adherence to time frame doesn't really matter. Lewis's

years in Chicago were consumed
with cold weather, strife and a
lot of time in court. Lewis fired
Lacy Banks, one African-American
columnist and hired Thom Greer,
another African-American
columnist. Both Banks and Greer
went on to illustrious journalism
careers. The courts upheld the
Sun-Times and Lewis in a
discrimination suit, though Banks
was later hired back at the paper.

In his lawsuit Banks hired a
rather flamboyant African-American
attorney, and Jim Minter traveled
north to serve as a character
witness for Lewis. In one
proceeding they called for Jim
Minter to come into the courtroom
for questioning. When the man took
a seat Lewis's attorney turned
around and paused. He said to
Lewis, "You did not tell me Jim
Minter is black." They sent in the
wrong person.

When the real Jim Minter took the stand Banks's attorney did everything he could to trip Jim up and depict Lewis as racist, without success. Again, the Sun-Times and Lewis prevailed in court.

While in Chicago Lewis confided to Jim that he never drove his car due to already crazy traffic made worse when it snowed. Lewis walked to and from work sockless in his Gucci loafers, at times needing to hold on to signposts to keep from getting blown away. Having lived in Chicago for 14 years I can attest that is not a formula for enjoyment of life there, regardless of what you do for a living. You dress for survival on the streets and change clothes for style once indoors. Especially footwear. In Chicago Gucci loafers can only sensibly be worn outdoors during a few days in August.

Despite all of the angst and turmoil, Jim told me the Chicago Sun-Times recognized Lewis's extraordinary talent. They offered to promote him to executive editor of the entire paper, representing a significant increase in, well, everything. It also represented that Lewis would have to commit to living in a city he could not stand for a whole lot longer than he wanted.

The Sun-Times top dog promotion offer was certainly news to me, but Lewis's appeal to Jim Minter for the chance to move back home was not. I asked Jim if I could explain my understanding, and he allowed me to tell it.

"Lewis asked you if he could come back to work for you, and you asked him to write five columns for your review." Again, I had read this somewhere.

Jim held up three fingers. Three columns, not five. Yes, they were good, and no, he no longer has them. Jim did not say so, but I expect the columns were only a formality. Jim wanted Lewis back as much as Lewis wanted to return. Except this time Lewis would return as a sports writer, not a sports editor. And this time it would be for the more liberal morning Constitution, not the more conservative evening Journal. But again, Lewis transitioning from sports to general humor and from editor to writer is where details get muddy.

Furman Bisher and Lewis did not get along well much of the time. Both had strong personalities, and at times one technically reported to the other. Sparks flew, but they mostly managed to stay out of each other's way.

Jim once made Furman an editor, a mistake he regretted, as that was not Furman's strength. He asked Furman to return to writing but let him keep the editor title.

Lewis, on the other hand, was a gifted editor and gifted columnist. When Jim had to leave town for major news stories he asked Lewis to edit the sports section. Jim often lamented the next day that Lewis did a better job of editing than Jim did. Yet I expect this is Jim's modesty and humility talking. The man becomes more of a hero by the minute.

Back to the race issue, only briefly. Late in life Lewis was on the waiting list for a heart transplant. When asked what he thought about the possibility of receiving the heart of a black donor, Lewis said, "That would be wonderful as long as he didn't go to Tech."

Lewis had to tolerate many bosses
sent down from the north to change
the style of the Atlanta
newspapers. Lewis was a specific
element of style those northern
bosses wanted to change - or
eliminate. Certain northerners
wanted Atlanta papers to be like
the New York Times, others wanted
something like USA Today. Lewis
saw the frequency of his columns
reduced. Atlanta paper staff
members collected columns they
knew would not run in Atlanta but
would likely run in distant
syndicated papers not so hoity
toity about journalistic style.
Lewis outlasted them all.

One such boss from Dayton Ohio was
with a group at dinner one night.
Also in the restaurant was Lewis
Grizzard. They caught each other's
eye, and Lewis approached the
table. As he was introduced around
Lewis offered to feel the legs of

a northern executive's wife. Lewis had written that northern women do not shave their legs but announced that the legs he briefly caressed were indeed freshly shaven. Only after Lewis departed did the wife confess that she had in fact not shaved her legs recently. Lewis was the master of tact when he needed to be, a quality he demonstrated that night. One can only imagine what Lewis could have said had he wanted to make that woman a stereotype of his theories on the grooming habits of northern women.

Jim opposed Lewis's syndication, fearing that Lewis would lose his focus on local southern appeal. Jim confesses he could not have been more wrong. Lewis stuck to his roots and readers as far away as Seattle voraciously consumed every word.

Jim a/k/a Mr. Minter reeled off
names of others I needed to
contact and some, very sadly,
recently deceased. Some are now
too old and frail, others
recovering from a hurricane, auto
accidents of their own and similar
unfortunate calamities. Jim
offered phone numbers for some and
introductions to those who would
need them before taking my call. I
wrote furiously. I have contacted
some and await replies from
others. Suffice it to say that
lunch with Jim Minter was a
pleasurable experience I will
treasure for life.

Rudy Connor

Rudy Connor makes BBQ Lewis would
have loved. If you Google "lewis
grizzard lake lanier" you will
find proof of it in search result
number 1 as of January 19, 2019
and for the last year running. It
is a September 2017 article I
wrote promoting Rudy's Smoky Q
restaurant at Bald Ridge Marina.
The only complaint I have about
Smoky Q is that's where I was
borrowing their WiFi while my
houseboat was sinking 5 minutes
away in October 2017. Let's not
get into that.

Rudy is a Lewis fan. Yet he is a graduate of the vile University of Alabama. That is only partially redeemed by the fact that he married Donna, a fine University of Georgia woman. The rest is redeemed by the fact that Rudy is not obnoxious during years when Bama upsets the Dawgs. That is pretty much every year except two or three since 1980.

Rudy was in a fraternity at Bama and performed feats that Lewis would like. When Rudy was a pledge the frat told him and fellow pledge brothers to go do some scavenger hunt type activities in Athens, Georgia. And Rudy did them.

The first was to climb naked, or nekkid, up the Sanford Stadium goalposts and get a picture doing it. Only Rudy and his goofball Bama buddies did not choose wisely when they chose where to get nekkid. They shed their clothes in the bleachers, then ran onto the field and up the goalpost. Mission accomplished, security lights came on and a bunch of guards started yelling and chasing. Nekkid Rudy and cohorts then had to exit hastily over hedges into the bleachers to fetch clothing, whereas clothing at the base of said goalposts would have been far more convenient and accessible. This exemplifies why it is so easy to gain admission to the University of Alabama.

The next feat Rudy and fellow pledges had to perform was to get a photo of themselves with Vince Dooley. This was far easier to accomplish than they expected. Dressed in neutral non Bama clothing, meaning they weren't wearing jorts or wife beater T-shirts, the crew just walked into the Athletic Association building.

When they got to Vince's office they raced past a receptionist and into the Coach's office. With minimal explanation they got a snapshot with smiling Vince and were gone.

In the modern era even UGA students can't get into the Athletic Association building without a retina scan and various liquid and solid DNA samples. If the entrant is from Alabama the trespasser is electronically vaporized along with any trace of evidence they ever existed on the planet. But that was then, and this is now.

If Rudy and pals had only waited a few decades I could have gotten them into Vince Dooley's living room. This exemplifies why it is so easy to gain admission to the University of Alabama.

Rudy and pledgemates completed other harmless scavenger hunt antics without getting arrested that neither he nor I can talk about. If you get the chance ask Rudy how many swings of a sledge axe it takes to remove a bulldog hood ornament from a Mack Truck 18 wheeler.

The punch line is when Rudy's crew returned to Tuscaloosa their elder brethren advised they did not really expect the young lads to perform any of those foolhardy tasks. It was simply a list of dares to test how foolhardy the young lads were. This exemplifies why it is so easy to gain admission to the University of Alabama.

Even Lewis would admire Rudy's exploits. Were Lewis around he may even choose to write a column about Rudy's exploits. Lewis liked to write about chaos, and hanging around Rudy and Smoky Q always promises some fun chaos. Not to mention killer BBQ.

Rudy's other attributes include very charming parents, Rudy Sr. a/k/a Big Rudy and Sally, even though both are Bama people. He also has a very attractive but unfortunately married sister. She lives in Chicago but occasionally beautifies Smoky Q with her charming presence when Rudy needs help. Smoky Q features a museum quality collection of international rock and roll memorabilia and music that Rudy personally assembled while he honed cooking skills in Switzerland. All of these things make Rudy more tolerable.

Rudy Conner is a funny, nice guy who makes great food, including BBQ, and Lewis Grizzard would have liked him. This being the case,

Rudy deserves a chapter, because I just wrote it.

New Years Eve

On New Year's Eve 1980 Lewis Grizzard was in the French Quarter, as was I. I did not see him there and do not know how I missed him. According to a recent firsthand account, Lewis approached a Lucky Dog vendor and offered to sell his product while the guy watched. The vendor declined, citing distrust, health code regulations and/or some combination thereof.

Lewis then offered to buy the whole cart for the night, complete with the inventory of Lucky Dogs. He probably paid the vendor his cost for a year, but Lewis only needed a few hours. That made distrust and health code issues go away. The vendor happily went away with a wad of cash.

Lewis sold Lucky Dogs all night
with typical Lewis flourish. A
large audience gathered around.
Then some lady ordered a Lucky Dog
with relish. Lewis advised her he
had no relish. The woman insisted
on relish. Lewis told her again
that he had no relish. She finally
said, "The Lucky Dog vendor at the
next corner has relish." To which
Lewis replied, "Lady, then take
your sorry 'arse' down to the next
corner and buy a Lucky Dog from
that guy." The woman was probably
a Yankee, though my source did not
confirm it.

During this time Lewis's wife
tired of the show and went back to
their hotel room for the night,
not in the best of spirits. She
evidently wished to spend her New
Years Eve doing something other
than watch Lewis sell Lucky Dogs.
When Lewis ran out of Lucky Dogs
at whatever hour, he walked with

my source and others back to their
hotel.

Lewis asked others to come talk to
his wife, as he was likely correct
in assuming she was not happy.
Others suggested she would be
asleep. Lewis agreed that made
sense, said good night and stepped
into the elevator alone. The
others stayed at lobby level to
chat a while longer.

Within 60 seconds the same
elevator door opened. Lewis was
still on it, with the elevator
phone in hand. He asked if anyone
in the party would kindly talk
some sense into his wife. Never in
the history of hotel elevator
telephones has one connected to a
guest room, and everyone knew it.

The others escorted Lewis up to
his room, watched him unlock the
door, go inside and close the door

behind him. They departed, hoping and praying Lewis would stay put for the night.

The next morning both Lewis and wife were perky and chipper at breakfast. Both were known to have amazing powers of resilience.

Tonight or tomorrow I will post Lewis's escapades the night of January 1, 1981 following Georgia's National Championship and celebration.

How I missed Lewis on 12/31/80 is a mystery, as my date and I roamed the entire French Quarter for hours. I am pretty sure I bought a few Lucky Dogs. Our 'just outside the Quarter' hotel was not the finest, and we postponed returning there until a few hours of slumber could be avoided no longer.

Dang, I wish I bought one of those Lucky Dogs from Lewis. I expensed part of that trip, as I visited a company office 2 days before or after the game. I would have asked the Lucky Dogs vendors for receipts. Had I asked Lewis for a receipt, he by error may have given me the one from the Lucky Dog vendor for the entire cart. I would now kill to have evidence of what he paid for that few hours of amusement.

Lewis took pride in accounting for unusual expenses, creatively justifying them and almost always receiving complete reimbursement. This caused dismay among some writers restricted to tighter travel allowances. Most of those were advised, "Sell as many papers as Lewis sells, then we will talk about your travel allowance."

I had far less success with
creative expense account
reimbursement, though it did not
prevent me from making valiant
attempts. In all probability I did
not generate a fraction of the
revenue for my employer as Lewis
did for his.

Wade Saye

Among the more difficult to find of Lewis's old friends was Wade Saye, a profound early influence in Lewis's career.

I found Wade via an unlikely connection, his first cousin once removed. Rob Saye is a photographer and writer for many outlets, including Bulldawg Illustrated, a great UGA periodical I recently discovered.

When I reached Rob I asked if by remote chance Wade is his dad. He replied, "No, he's my dad's cousin." That's how these things are playing out.

Records suggest Lewis first wrote for the upstart Athens Daily News during his freshman year at UGA. That is incorrect. Lewis first wrote at the decades old Athens Banner-Herald. Wade Saye is the reason Lewis moved to the Daily News.

In 1965 the Banner-Herald was rather moribund, another word Lewis would know but I had to look up to make sure I am using it right. The elder Banner-Herald was dull, leaving opportunity for creative folks at the Daily News to create a competing paper. Per Wade, they launched with high hopes on June 19.

The Daily News needed credibility and Wade Saye would give them that. They offered to double his salary from $50 to $100 per week to entice him. Wade accepted and did the proper thing in the day by giving the Banner-Herald his two week notice. Wade gave me names of the guys who did this, but I will not knock them lest they still have relatives who are Bulldogs: The Banner-Herald publisher and editor told Wade he could depart Friday. They had already found his replacement.

They point here is the Banner-Herald scoffed at both the Daily News and Wade's decision to risk everything by joining a publication that stood no chance of survival vs the veritable and illustrious benchmark.

The Daily News went on to kick the Banner-Herald's arse. One reason is that Wade recommended to Daily

News founders Claude Williams, publisher, and Glenn Vaughn, editor, that they also hire the talented young writer who worked with or for Wade, Lewis Grizzard. With Chuck Perry (discussed elsewhere), society page writer Colleen Kelly and photographer Brownie Stevens, Wade and Lewis outworked and outperformed anyone and everyone at the Banner-Herald. They became known as "the people's paper", covering local Athens from high schools to … a black bear sighted in a local suburb. Athens loved it, and the newspaper world took notice.

Wade Saye officially began as the Daily News sports editor, with Lewis as writer covering high school sports. No one was much hung up on titles. Wade soon took over editing the entire paper, and Lewis took over sports. The entire staff worked tirelessly with passion, amazing even themselves with their success.

Re the newspaper world taking notice, Augusta's Morris Communications soon bought the Banner-Herald, followed shortly thereafter by overtures to buy the Daily News. Claude Williams and Glenn Vaughn resisted early overtures to which staff were not privy. They were too busy cranking out a great product.

Soon Williams and Vaughn accepted an offer to their liking, and the expectation was that the Banner-Herald would absorb the Daily News. As devoted as staff were to Williams and Vaughn, they were heartbroken by the news. They each felt they had built a stake in an enterprise they hoped to continue to build. The thought of joining the rather snooty Banner-Herald, even if there was wholesale change in leadership, appealed to no one at the Daily News. Not one person stayed on for more than a month or so.

Brownie Davis went on to careers working "over 100 jobs" according to Wade, including a lucrative stint at some poultry publication. That strikes me as an unusual outlet for a gifted photographer. But chickens are big business. If you find a good niche, go for it.

I am still looking for Colleen Kelly. I have not begun to look for any Mark Smith. If you find him let me know, but I only want the correct Mark Smith. Claude Williams and Glenn Vaughn each went on to celebrated publishing careers and died in 2018. I regret missing the opportunity to talk to them, as many have advised they were two great newspaper minds.

Wade went on to an esteemed career with newspapers in Columbus and

Marietta GA, Covington Kentucky
and finally Knoxville Tennessee.
He is happily retired in
Knoxville, where he only rarely
takes grief for remaining a loyal
Bulldog.

We pretty much know what Lewis
Grizzard went on to do. Or maybe
we are continuing here to try and
explain it.

Readers of America, you can thank
Wade Saye for bringing you Lewis
Grizzard.

Chuck Perry

Stoddard note: Chuck Perry was kind to edit his own chapter. My original draft had Lewis writing briefly for the Athens Daily Herald, then following Wade Saye to the Athens Daily News. That was per Wade's account. No other info I have seen shows Lewis having first written for the Banner-Herald. If Wade is correct, it may have only been for a week, day or cup of coffee.

I will not dispute guys like Chuck or Wade, who have each forgotten more about journalism than I will ever learn. I let their accounts speak for themselves.

It would be excellent to have each media legend edit their own chapter. Yet if I asked such busy or formerly busy people to do that this may not publish before 2037.

Thus, I am most grateful for one such chapter.

From this point forward is Chuck's edited version:

Lewis began his newspaper career while a freshman at UGA. He was an occasional stringer for the Atlanta Journal sports department, covering mostly minor sports. He soon joined the staff of the upstart Athens Daily News when sports editor Wade Saye recognized the young talent. See separate chapter on Wade Saye.

Lewis later promoted Chuck Perry's career in much the same way that Wade promoted Lewis's career.

The Athens Daily News, which labeled itself "The People Paper," was an outgrowth of the Athens Advertiser – not much more than what its name implied, a paper full of ads. Owner/Publisher Claude Williams and Editor Glenn

Vaughan saw an opportunity to create something special in the Athens market at a time when the decades-old Athens Banner-Herald (formed in 1921) was rather lethargic at best. When they launched the Daily News in 1965, Athens became the smallest town in America with two competing newspapers. The Daily News was soon challenging the Banner-Herald in terms of both circulation and in town buzz.

Claude Williams initially hired Chuck Perry, still a student and athlete at Athens High School, for mailroom duties, which included operation of the addressograph machine that got papers properly labeled for delivery to the growing list of subscribers.

After graduation in 1966, Chuck entered UGA with a partial baseball scholarship, but he soon realized his competition was such that he may never get either a full scholarship or much, if any, playing time. He turned his effort to full-time academics and part-time work at the Daily News.

Seeing how hard Chuck worked, and perhaps sympathetic because Lewis too had started UGA with limited financial means, Lewis aspired to get his friend Chuck out of the mailroom. When Wade Saye became managing editor of the Daily News, Lewis moved up to sports editor and hired Chuck to take his spot as the staff sportswriter.

Chuck commented that the Daily News launched at a time when sports at the high school and UGA levels were more exciting than the city of Athens itself. Publisher Williams and Editor Vaughn seized on that with a sports focus and around-town news made exciting by lively writing. For example, a black bear sighting on the outskirts of town captivated Daily News readers for a few days, while the Banner-Herald scoffed at such frivolity making print news. Athens readers ate it up and came to love the Daily News.

Along the way, Lewis lured his Moreland high school sweetheart to Athens. She was then in Atlanta enrolled in modeling school, and even the shortened distance was more than Lewis could take. She took a job at the Daily News staffing the reception desk and performing office tasks. Lewis and she married at age 19.

Young Lewis and young Chuck also developed a fondness for golf that neither of them could afford from the perspective of either money or time. On Mondays they occasionally got permission to play on the otherwise closed (for maintenance) Athens Country Club course. One particular stuffed-shirt member would invariably challenge their presence on course, chastising them for being non-members trying to sneak on. Charming guy.

The Athens Daily News finally threatened the Banner-Herald's position in Athens to the point that its owner, Augusta-based Morris Communications, bought out the Daily News in December 1967. The two papers merged but much of the Daily News' "fire in the belly" was doused.

About that time, Atlanta Journal sports editor Jim Minter hired Lewis as his assistant. Lewis left UGA prior to graduation but couldn't pass up the opportunity to work with Minter and sports columnist Furman Bisher. Chuck became sports editor of the Banner-Herald. Upon graduation from UGA, he went into the U.S. Army briefly and returned as Associate Editor of the Banner-Herald while he earned a Masters Degree in English.

When Jim Minter was promoted to Managing Editor of the Atlanta Constitution, Lewis became Journal sports editor and once again sought Chuck as his assistant. Chuck started work in the Journal sports department in 1974.

After a painful divorce from wife No. 1, Lewis met wife No. 2 at the Journal-Constitution. Chuck recalled that they were married on a train. This was the first I heard of Lewis combining his love of trains and women. In fact, they were married on short-notice at step brother Ludlow Porch's house and then immediately boarded a train for their honeymoon.

Back to Lewis and Chuck and the stuffed shirt Athens golf guy who reminded them they were not members of the club. Chuck reports that after Lewis became a national sensation, he went on to join many golf clubs, including the Athens Country Club. Tony Privett,

Lewis's business manager at the time, advised Lewis he could likely walk onto about any golf course in the country as a celebrity guest. No, Lewis wanted full membership, likely due to insults from that Athens stuffed shirt. It got to the point that Privett scolded him. "Lewis, you are about to break the 14 club rule!"

It did not take long for even duffer me to understand. Golfers can carry a maximum of 14 clubs in their bag. Lewis tried to push a similar limit on the number of country clubs he could join.

On to early lessons learned in Athens and continued in Atlanta. As mentioned in another chapter, Lewis once missed a famous flea-flicker football play where UGA beat Alabama. As sports editor of the Journal, he dispatched a poor reporter to stand in an Atlanta stadium restroom and interview patrons while they missed Hank Aaron's historic 715th home run. Chuck does not recall who drew the short straw for that assignment.

From his People Paper days in Athens, Lewis was always fond of stories that related to common sports fans. What mattered most to them? So he often sent reporters to sit in barbershops and pick up on what patrons were talking about while waiting or getting clipped themselves.

When it was rumored that Atlanta Hawks great "Pistol Pete" Maravich might be entertaining offers from other teams, Lewis sent a reporter to stake out Pete's house to see where he went that day. Not with an intrusive photographer or anything. This was before paparazzi was even a word.

As with many things in Lewis's career, roles later reversed. After years in the newspaper business, Chuck moved on to book publishing, where he published many of Lewis's books at Peachtree Publishers and Longstreet Press.

Such is how friendships and legends are made.

Shelton Stevens

In early conversations several
friends of Lewis said I needed to
talk to Shelton Stevens. Based on
what they told me I agreed but
thought that might be difficult,
as Shelton is a pretty busy guy.
Then I learned Shelton is a
formerly pretty busy guy.

Shelton retired in 2017 after 25
years as Executive Director of
Children's Healthcare of Atlanta.
There he helped raise hundreds of
millions of dollars to help sick

kids. Work does not get much more noble than that.

Via Google search you can find the "Shelton Stevens, CHOA (Retirement Video)" on Vimeo, an incredible 26 minutes on a great man's career and selflessness.

Shelton also happens to be Lewis's UGA Sigma Pi fraternity brother, former roommate and lifelong friend.

Two of the guys who said I should talk to Shelton were Mark Reed, another of Lewis's fraternity brothers, and John "Chomper" Chambers, my own UGA Phi Gamma Delta fraternity brother. It was Mark who eventually got me Shelton's contact information. Chomper is relatively ADHD and entirely useless, though he was once Shelton's next door neighbor. This was before Shelton got smart and moved away from Chomper and

Chomper proved his uselessness by moving to Alabama.

Once I succeeded in reaching Shelton he invited me to coffee at his house on December 6, 2018. I figured a guy who led such an exemplary life would have nothing but clean, highly publishable stories to share. Wrong. Only about 15% of what Shelton offered was family friendly Lewis content, yet it was too priceless to not publish without a little cleaning up.

Children of America, please understand all this stuff happened long ago, and Shelton did not initiate any of it. He just told it, and I am just writing it. Shelton is not responsible for what is written here. Nor am I. No one is responsible for any of this.

There was a guy by the name of
Archer Brandon "Bugar" Seeley in
Albany GA who was even funnier
than Lewis Grizzard. Bugar, his
wife Betsy Ann, and other notables
often partied with Lewis in
Athens, Albany and elsewhere. At
one gathering at the Sheeley's
Albany home then UGA basketball
coach Hugh Durham or his wife
Malinda asked Bugar if the ceiling
fans on their poolside veranda
helped make the summer heat
bearable.

Bugar replied, "No, Betsy Ann and
I like to skinny dip. The ceiling
fans are to keep gnats off of
Betsy Ann's (blank)." Where you
see (blank) insert the term of
your choice for an intimate part
of the female anatomy where the
sun don't typically shine.

According to Shelton, the Durhams,
Vince and Barbara Dooley and
others may or may not have left

the veranda. Whether or not it was to compose themselves or not be seen laughing at such a raucous comment is left to conjecture. Unfortunately Bugar and Betsy Ann are deceased and can not be reached for comment.

At the Ponte Vedra, Florida home of other friends Lewis, Shelton and significant others gathered before a Georgia Florida game. Participants discussed here are still living and therefore shall remain nameless. One afternoon Shelton, Lewis and a still surviving 3rd person had been overserved at a golf course or similar and needed to get home. The only non drinker was "Blind Reggie", who, as his nickname would suggest, could not see. Or therefore drive. They did not have but about a quarter mile to go, so Shelton and Lewis coerced Reggie to drive at a speed not to exceed 5 miles per hour while one of them

navigated and/or held the wheel.
The mystery man owner of the
vehicle was entirely unconscious
in the back seat.

After Reggie hit three mailboxes
despite all of the navigational
and steering assistance, they
parked the car on a shoulder and
walked the rest of the way home.
The next morning mystery man's
wife found their damaged car mere
steps from the driveway and
demanded an explanation from her
husband. To this day he does not
know Blind Reggie was behind the
wheel - and not him.

Children of America, do not try
this at home. Such activity was
once legal and even condoned in
the greater Jacksonville Florida
metropolitan area decades ago the
week prior to the Georgia Florida
game. I know, because for several
consecutive years I saw people in
police uniform stand around and

not direct traffic, provide
parking lot suggestions or similar
functions law enforcement people
should perform while being paid.

That is why they called it the
"World's Largest Outdoor Adult
Beverage Party". Then they tried
to stop calling it that, but
everyone still called it that. So
"they" gave up. At least now the
police do their job and far fewer
100% visually impaired people get
behind the wheel.

Law enforcement non performance
was apparently not limited to
state or city employees. I was
once at a Fernandina Beach marina
when a yacht owner docked and
inquired where he could find a
federal customs official to check
him in. A local replied, "After
the Georgia Florida game." This
was three days before said game.

But enough about me. Back to Lewis. And Shelton.

On the eve of the University of Georgia's 1980 National Championship victory over Notre Dame in New Orleans, Lewis commandeered a French Quarter Lucky Dog stand and sold Lucky Dogs all night. Read that account elsewhere in this book. It was also New Year's Eve. No chance for Big Easy mischievous activity on a night like that.

The night celebrating Georgia's National Championship was spent in the suite of Barbara and Vince Dooley. Those in attendance included Macon Telegraph Sports Editor Harley Bowers, Shelton, Lewis and their wives or significant others. Nothing but respectable behavior ensued, as the hostess and host were Barbara and Vince Dooley. But the respectable behavior did not end

until around 3 AM. What a joy that
story was to hear.

On the other hand, my significant
other and I lodged at a dodgy
"near the quarter" no-tell motel
that evening.

Shelton and Lewis participated in
a number of charitable
invitational golf tournaments.
Benefactors included, but were not
limited to, Scottish Rite,
Eggleston and Children's
Healthcare Network. Venues
included, but were not limited to,
Atlanta Country Club, Big Canoe
and the King and Prince. Themes
included, but were not limited to,
8 Hours of Golf, Smart Ass White
Boys and Gator Haters.

Participants included, but were
not limited to, Furman Bisher,
Andrew Young, Ron Hudspeth, Jodie
Powell and Hamilton Jordan.

At one such event the most coveted competition was for the Dead Ass Last Award. The recipient got The Boobie Prize, a set of Boobies he was forced/entitled to strap on for the duration of the following year's tournament.

During that era I played at Chicago public courses like Sydney R. Marovitz a/k/a Waveland with the likes of Ross Zwerling. Greens fee for 9 holes was $9 and tee times reserved by Ticketmaster. I easily could have qualified for any Lewis tournament Dead Ass Last Award had I been invited, which I wasn't. And I could have taken a lot longer than 8 hours to win it.

Shelton put me in touch with Georgia Tech legend Pepper Rodgers, who almost made a Tech fan out of Lewis. Read that account elsewhere in this book.

At the behest of Vince Dooley, in 1978 Lewis coached the Black team and WSB's Phil Schaefer coached the Red team at the UGA spring game. I would have been a junior. If I attended I do not remember it, and for this I kick myself. Thanks to Lewis's superior coaching skills and a tailback named Willie McClendon the Black team prevailed 24-0. Lewis's halftime pep talk was noteworthy in that it included an order for beer.

We are not going in chronological order here because Shelton did not talk in chronological order. During the 1965 opening game against national champion Alabama Lewis was at the concession stand making a bourbon and Coke during the infamous Flea Flicker touchdown play that enabled the Dawgs to prevail 18-17. Thereafter, at every Sanford Stadium game Lewis attended during his undergraduate years Sigma Pi pledges were dispatched to make Lewis's drinks. I will leave it to readers' imagination to speculate how Lewis rid himself of byproducts from those drinks. It may have to do with some contraption described in the Jim Minter chapter.

There is really no good way to close the Shelton Stevens chapter, as he referred me to many others who told Lewis stories that bring me back to questions I have yet to ask Shelton. Maybe for the next book.

Let's close with the classic and mythical "Greatest Headline in the History of Sports Journalism". Lewis never wrote it. Shelton did. It goes like this:

"Dogs to Play Cocks With Dicks Out"

Sorry children of America. No way to clean this one up.

Georgia had a linebacker by the name of Robert "Happy" Dicks, who went on to become a prestigious physician. Happy was injured and perhaps unable to play in a game vs a certain opponent. That opponent may or may not have been the University of South Carolina, familiarly known as Gamecocks. Cockfighting is the state sport of South Carolina, but let's not get into that.

You can Google all this and get multiple explanations, including articles by people who claim to have read it all in their morning paper. Many accounts are full of misinformation or outright lies, though the statute of limitations on such matters has long since expired.

Legend has it that newly married Lewis popped into his former Callaway Gardens apartment after a day of school and work to tell his former roommates that the editor at the newspaper for which he wrote 'took drunk'. If the column Lewis submitted escaped the editor's attention, the next day readers would awaken to the Greatest Headline in the History of Sports Journalism.

Shelton was one of those former roommates, as was Jerry "Bake" Baker, who I will get to in another chapter.

Maybe Lewis did pop in after work, but he didn't write anything like that earlier in the day. Former roommates kicked around some ideas, and Shelton commenced to writing. It may not have even been before a South Carolina game, because Shelton's initial version made no reference to that school's

semi-obscene abbreviated mascot.
Shelton simply wrote "Dogs to Play
With D---ks Out. See, I'm trying
to make this family friendly.

Someone later added C--ks because
they thought it was funnier. They
were right. But facts get skewed
even from there. Jim Minter
recalls it as "Dogs to Play Vols
With D--ks Out". Who am I to argue
with either Jim Minter or Shelton
Stevens? You can argue with either
or both of them all you want.

I just tell the stories as they
are told to me.

Ernie Cain & Jere Mills

After meeting with Shelton Stevens I dashed to meet with a cohort who met Lewis later in life. Can't recall how I knew my UGA acquaintance Ollie Kennon is a member of Lewis's Ansley Golf Club, but Ollie seems to know everyone. I asked him to ask elder members and staff if anyone recalled Lewis. Ollie reported Ansley had a new, rather young general manager. Dang it. I waited.

Shortly thereafter Ollie delivered Gold. Mounted somewhere on an Ansley Golf Club wall is this framed uncashed check for a gambling debt written to Lewis, apparently one of many like it that he never cashed. It did not take long to find the issuer of that check, Ernie Cain.

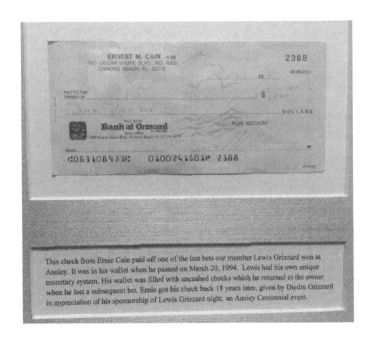

This check from Ernie Cain paid off one of the last bets our member Lewis Grizzard won at Ansley. It was in his wallet when he passed on March 20, 1994. Lewis had his own unique monetary system. His wallet was filled with uncashed checks which he returned to the owner when he lost a subsequent bet. Ernie got his check back 18 years later, given by Diedra Grizzard in appreciation of his sponsorship of Lewis Grizzard night, an Ansley Centennial event.

When I phoned Ernie he remembered donating the check to Ansley but did not know it was on display there. He proposed that we meet for lunch at the Club to both talk and look for his check. When we finally agreed on a day, meeting at his home was more convenient.

Ernie lives in my hometown of Sandy Springs. When I got to his house I learned I grew up on the wrong side of the tracks. I never knew spreads like his existed within my district. He even sent one of his kids to my Ridgeview high school, now demoted to a middle school. His daughter graduated a few years after my time.

I met Ernie before establishing the habit of taking selfies with interview subjects. This photo of him with a Gator Hater Tournament championship trophy will have to suffice. I expect few if any complaints from folks who will get sick of seeing me.

Ernie is a self-made guy in the steel business, and at 79 still works that business. Though his family were early Atlanta real estate investors and for that matter, steel company executives, nothing was handed to Ernie. He started laboring in the mill and worked his way up the ranks before founding his own company.

Ernie recalls first meeting Lewis circa 1989 after a late night gin rummy competition. At about 1:30 AM Ernie offered to give Lewis a lift home, not far from that competition. When Ernie asked where Lewis lived Lewis replied, "I don't know. Just start driving." They successfully found Lewis's home, and Ernie did not depart until he saw Lewis enter safely and closed the door behind him.

Lewis and Ernie quickly bonded at Ansley, and they golfed together across the country. Ernie accompanied Lewis to Las Vegas when he was the opening act for stars like Randy Travis. On one trip Lewis's contingent occupied 18 guest rooms. Lewis once pulled an all nighter before performing at 9 PM. Sleep deprived, he was not his usual brilliant and humorous self. His agent strongly urged Lewis to not make a habit of all nighters. Lewis performed the next three nights without a hitch, and the off night was quickly forgotten.

Lewis often bounced ideas off of Ernie, polishing them for a column the next day. Like many, Ernie said Lewis faithfully began is writing day no later than 5:30 AM regardless of what he did the night before.

Ernie recalled a White Trash Invitational golf tournament, though he may have been thinking of the Smart Ass White Boys charity even mentioned elsewhere. As I've said, I will not split hairs with my elders when they are telling stories on a roll. Ernie also recalled a Pig Valve Open tournament, which no one else I have spoken to has yet mentioned.

After Lewis became an early homeowner at Lake Oconee he invited more and more friends there to golf, gamble and get into general mischief. Ernie grew so fond of Oconee he bought the house next door to Lewis. He still owns it, though he advises that Lewis's house has been considerably enlarged and altered since Lewis's days.

Ernie's house served as lodging for actor Joe Pesci when "My Cousin Vinny" filmed in the area.

Too bad the area was off limits to homeowners - who were obviously rewarded - during the filming. What Lewis may have written about interaction with Pesci would have been quite an interesting read.

Lewis and Ernie traveled far and wide together, often with Lewis's beloved driver James Shannon behind the wheel. On one such occasion Lewis waxed poetic:

"Ernie, we may be the only two people in America riding down an Interstate listening to World War II music playing gin rummy in a stretch limousine while heading to a golf course. Life is good."

At Ansley Ernie recalls an incident when one of Lewis's girlfriends or fiancées attempted to charge something to Lewis's account. She was declined as her name was not authorized on the account. When Lewis approached the clubhouse after a round of golf his significant other confronted him with, "Do you join as a single man?!" When Lewis offered no quick answer the lady punched him. Ernie can not recall if Lewis's Ansley membership predated his romance to that woman.

Ernie made the rounds with Lewis in Buckhead and beyond, including Harrison's with Pete the Northside Barkeep, Longhorn Steaks with George McKerrow and numerous haunts in states other than Georgia.

Ernie was best man at Lewis's 4th wedding days before his final surgery. He was one of two best men actually, as Lewis had arranged a backup just in case. Ernie lifted the frail Lewis out of his wheelchair so he could take his vows.

Back to Ernie's gambling check, Ernie recalled it to be the only check he ever wrote to Lewis. Lewis lost wagers more often than he won - at cards, golf or whatever, and he almost always paid his debts in cash.

Speaking of gambling, a deceased cohort of Ernie and Lewis who we shall dub "Arty" to protect the privacy of his next of kin, was property manager of several Lake Oconee homes with absentee owners far and wide. Arty hosted poker nights at lakefront homes he managed but did not own. Nor did he have the owner's permission to host such events. See chapter on Carey Williams.

I had other reasons to head toward the Lake Oconee vicinity soon, and I asked Ernie if anyone still in the area might have known Lewis. For instance, a newspaper editor or real estate agent. Ernie mentioned Carey Williams as a news guy and Jere Mills as the only Oconee agent who was likely there during Lewis's days. Ernie also gave me the address of his Oconee home so I could do a drive by. He advised few if any of his neighbors would be there this time of year, including the current owners of Lewis's house.

I thought to ask if maybe I could host a Poker Night for old times' sake, then I recalled asking homeowner permission was not how that used to work.

Sure enough, only days later I traveled for real estate business to Milledgeville, just south of Lake Oconee. On a free afternoon I trekked north for a glance at Ernie's home and Lewis's former home. GPS led me to a Reynolds Lake Oconee security gate. When I announced the purpose for my visit the guard said he would have to

phone Ernie. I concurrently phoned
Ernie, got his voicemail and left
the message, "Ernie, you gave me
the address but did not tell me I
would need security clearance to
get to your house. The Reynolds
guard is probably also leaving you
a message, so please call one or
both of us to gain me admittance.
Thanks."

The guard politely confirmed he
left a message for Ernie but could
not admit me without owner
permission. I understood that,
though I had nothing else to do
and no idea how soon Ernie might
get back to us. I decided to head
16 miles southwest to the nearest
library in Eatonton. After a few
minutes in the library it dawned
on me that I am a real estate
broker. Real estate brokers can
get passes into almost anywhere.

I had not yet had enough caffeine.
I hauled back 16 miles to the

Reynolds real estate office. I introduced myself and asked if Jere Mills was in. He was not, but the desk agent gave me an entrance pass. By the time I got back to the security gate Ernie had called and authorized the guard to not shoot me. The guard gave me a second entry pass, this one personalized with Ernie's name. I now have two authorizations to enter Reynolds Lake Oconee. With a little Liquid Paper perhaps I can fudge the dates and go host that poker night.

I drove by Ernie's and Lewis's places. As Ernie suggested no neighbors appeared to be home. If only the walls on Lewis's abode could talk, I would ask a lot of questions. But I did not know which were Lewis's original walls or later expansion walls, so I departed.

I called Jere Mills and scheduled coffee the next morning. Not only was Jere around Oconee when Lewis was alive, Lewis was the reason Jere is at Oconee. Jere is a former Atlantan and current member of Ansley Golf Club. He was one of many who Lewis invited to Oconee. Jere liked it so much he stayed and prospered as a leading real estate agent. Lewis, Ernie and Jere golfed together often at both Ansley and Oconee.

I expect Jere has a collection of Lewis golf tournament trophies too, but he did not haul any from his office to our meeting room that day. I should have asked.

Why did Ernie not tell me these things? I keep getting information in bits and pieces. It would be great if someone would just give me complete context so I don't sound like an idiot when I start asking questions. I guess that adds to the fun.

Jere informed me of yet another Lewis related golf tournament, the Moreland National. I find no golf course via Google search in Moreland, so it must have taken place in Newnan or Hogansville. The incident Jere described at the Moreland National was Lewis persistently flirting with a beer and sandwich girl at the 10th hole refreshments shed. No surprise there.

Ernie and Jere are two surviving foursome members of a remarkable round of golf involving Lewis. After Lewis's 3rd surgery his left index fingertip remained black. On this outing Lewis was partnered with "Arty". referenced earlier. Lewis and Arty were down a bunch of money to Ernie and Jere. The tip of Lewis's index finger fell off. Arty wanted to rush Lewis to the hospital under the pretense that he needed urgent medical attention. This would also traditionally nullify any debt, since the players in debt would be deprived the opportunity to reverse their fortune. Lewis, Ernie and Jere blew Arty off. Jere suggested that Lewis use the fingertip as a unique ball marker once they reached the green.

And Lewis did so.

Not sure if my notes are correct, but Jere may have said #7 on that course is still informally known by many as the "finger hole".

On Saturday night I was back in Milledgeville thinking about church the next day. I gave thought to calling Jere to ask where he went, but that would be a bit intrusive given I had only met him once. I looked online and was about to opt for First Presbyterian. Then Lake Oconee Church caught my eye. I was pleasantly amazed to learn it was a branch of my North Point Church, some 100 miles east. I read that Lake Oconee Church meets in a cineplex until construction of their permanent campus is completed in March.

Sunday morning I took a front row end seat, as I was minutes late, the room was dark and my eyes had not yet adjusted. Moments later a familiar looking guy passed in front of me with a lady. My eyes may have still been wonky, but he looked a lot like Jere Mills. I asked an usher, and he confirmed it to be Jere. I followed up the steps, shook Jere's hand with a whispered reintroduction and took a seat one row in front. Throughout the service I wondered if Jere thought I had been stalking him for a couple of days.

Over coffee after the service I met Jere's wife Bebe and spilled to them that my being there that day was an 11th hour change in plans. We marveled over the coincidence of it all. Not only did Jere go to that church, he and Bebe happened to pick one of the many screen rooms I happened to pick. Oconee Church members fill almost all of them, especially around Christmas.

After Jere and Bebe departed for family holiday festivities I lingered with volunteers Chad Pigg and Dan Kramer. They were youngish guys but familiar with Lewis. I asked them to ask around about elder church members who may have a Lewis story to share. Jere is pondering the same on my behalf, but he may not know recent arrivals from Atlanta with Lewis experiences unrelated to Oconee. I try to plant seeds everywhere.

From church I drove to plant seeds at the Ritz-Carlton Reynolds, Lake Oconee, which was built long after Lewis's days. I met with staff there who expressed interest in my return to talk about this book upon completion. I assured them I can tailor a 20 minute talk to a family friendly or adults only audience, followed by Q&A that can last for up to several decades as long as lodging is included at the Ritz-Carlton Reynolds, Lake Oconee.

That last offer stands for the Waldorf Astoria in New York, Drake in Chicago and St. Regis in San Francisco. You can keep Las Vegas.

I promise to do zero damage to any room in which I lodge with the exception of Vegas.

If anyone makes me go to Vegas again I promise nothing.

Carey Williams

As mentioned too many times elsewhere, if you Google "lewis grizzard lake lanier" the number one result is something I wrote in 2017. That is not because of my brilliant writing or savvy search engine optimization. It is because Lewis apparently spent little time on Lanier. Lewis was a Lake Oconee guy.

If you Google "lewis grizzard lake oconee" the number one result for quite some time and as of this writing, January 19, 2019, is this guy, Carey Williams.

The result should be a short video of Carey talking about Lewis and Lake Oconee area antics. You can't miss him. He looks just like the guy on the right above except he is moving and talking.

Carey and Mickey Mantle are the two main reasons Lewis bought a Lake Oconee house only a couple of years after they filled the lake. Lewis first came to the area to enjoy adult beverages with Mickey and eventually play golf at Harbor Club, an early course before there was a Reynolds, Ritz-Carlton or any highfalutin stuff.

Carey is the second generation owner-publisher of the Greensboro Herald Journal, a robust Oconee area community paper. As newspapermen Lewis and Carey took an immediate liking to one another. Carey claims to have written the only column that Lewis ever reprinted verbatim, about a guy named Pip Stone, a farmer who avoided getting killed by not going to his property on a day when the place was getting robbed. God told Pip not to go, but Pip did not find out until the next day why God kept him away.

Maybe there were times Lewis did not want to go home, and if he reprinted Carey's Pip article God would give Lewis clearer instructions and excuses for some wife.

Carey is responsible for finding Lewis's devoted driver, James Shannon. Carey got James to drive Lewis for a single ride, but Lewis kept James on for 11 years. You can see that story on the video. Many have suggested I speak to James. Sadly he passed away in 1995, only a year after Lewis.

In the 1980s Mickey Mantle took a
$100,000 per year job at an
Atlantic City casino to greet and
play golf with customers. That was
his highest salary when he was
playing baseball, the Jersey gig
required a lot less work. Yet it
forced him to sever ties to the
New York Yankees and major league
baseball.

Mickey was free to continue paid
appearances at golf tournaments.
He attended a charity event at
Harbor Club and liked both the
course and the weather. Both were
a refreshing change to what he
experienced in the Northeast, so
he decided to stay a while. Soon
Mickey's friends like Whitey Ford
and Billy Martin started to pop
down for visits. Not long
thereafter Lewis fell in with that
crowd. Perhaps his fondness for
those pretty entertaining fellows
is why Lewis talked about places

like Chicago and Cleveland when he
disparaged Yankees.

There was a gentleman, now
deceased, who was friends with
many of the above, though not
nearly as affluent. One of his
businesses was caretaking for
absentee owners of seasonal Lake
Oconee properties. In that
position he knew when owners might
be present or in, for instance,
Asia. The gentleman used that
information to host elaborate
casino nights at million dollar
residences that cost him nothing.
In fact, he was paid to not use
such residences and make sure no
one but the owners used them. But
that was rather limiting.

Let's call the deceased gentleman
Arty, because he may still have
relatives in the area. Arty would
arrange for security guards to
stand outside such events, not to
guard against burglars, but to

guard against owners should they unexpectedly show up unannounced from some place such as Asia. They were supposed to give Arty advance notice of their visit so he could ensure their residence was neat and tidy for their arrival. But sometimes owners of four and five resort homes can be surprisingly discourteous and disobedient.

There was not much concern that the sheriff's office might show up to these casino nights, as most nights the sheriff was winning or losing money inside the very residence Arty found conveniently available that week.

Were the FBI to show up, which they were unlikely to do in 1980s Putnam County Georgia without cause, they would find local law enforcement already on the case with a bunch of celebrities on their way to or already inducted in Cooperstown. Unless someone got

killed the FBI would have few
qualms, and this was not like
meetings in Apalachin New York,
where attendees were a whole lot
more likely to start gunplay. Even
criminal trespass would not be a
federal issue, and Arty probably
had official looking documents
giving everyone permission to be
there.

For purposes of past sheriff
exoneration, Lake Oconee also
borders Morgan and Greene
Counties. That at least spreads
out the possibilities as to which
of several sheriffs may or may not
have maintained law and order and
kept the peace at Arty's casino
nights.

Arty not only accepted money from
homeowners to prevent strangers
from entering their premises, he
also charged strangers a fee to
enter casino night premises they
were not supposed to enter. On top

of that he often dealt cards, as
he could not afford the
substantial stakes wagered per
hand, much less over the course of
many hours. On more than one
occasion "the house" ran out of
money with Arty dealing, meaning
funds mysteriously made its way
into the hands of someone other
than folks actually playing cards.

In other words, Arty was skimming.
One almost gets lost in the math
trying to figure out if this was
triple or quadruple dipping. In a
place like Apalachin Arty might
find himself sleeping with fishes,
especially with a deep lake right
out the back door. But without
Arty the fellows might have to
rent a VFW hall or something for
such casino nights, and those in
Putnam County were often booked
weekends in advance for bingo or
Boy Scout meetings. Arty got a
pass, even if it meant issuing

credit for cover charges at some future casino night.

In case anyone wondered, Lewis was in attendance at most of the aforementioned casino nights. He almost certainly told stories. If those I talked to are to be believed, Lewis lost money more often than he won. Lewis was not a great card player, as adult beverage consumption may have interfered with his judgment.

Back to James Shannon and Lewis. Once the two bonded it meant Lewis did not have to concern himself with driving combined with adult beverages. James did not touch adult beverages, creating an ideal partnership.

Thus, whether on back roads or highways Lewis might ask James to "take it to 100". James was a skilled driver, and Lewis liked to get to destinations quick. On one

such occasion James was pulled
over. The law enforcement officer
asked James to follow him to the
station. Instead of calling a
lawyer James called Carey
Williams. Carey asked James which
station he was visiting and to
please put the highest ranking
official on the phone. Carey and
the high ranking official had a
brief conversation and arrived at
an expedient solution. Carey drove
to the station in question.

Upon arrival Carey witnessed as
the law enforcement official semi-
officially deputized an overserved
Lewis Grizzard, complete with
oversized badge and official
looking documents. Armed with such
credentials, James and Lewis never
received a single citation for the
duration of their years together.
This despite "taking it to 100"
often and getting pulled over
often. The unnamed law enforcement
agency, their badge and ad hoc

documents obviously carried considerable clout.

With local Greene County High competing for the 1993 football state championship Lewis Grizzard had agreed to perform the ceremonial coin flip. When Lewis found himself committed elsewhere he asked Carey and others if it would be okay for Mickey Mantle to sub for him. Others thought they heard Lewis wrong but Carey knew he heard him right. Mickey would indeed flip a coin. Only problem was at game time Mickey had been overserved to the point someone needed to drive him onto the field. He wobbled out of a vehicle, flipped a coin, waved, wobbled back into a vehicle and departed. The crowd roared. Fortunately no one scheduled a Mickey speech.

For the record Greene County defeated Mary Parsons 24-21 to

take the crown. You can find the
team photo on the wall of Carey's
Greensboro Herald Journal office.
Doubtful that Mickey Mantle wrote
a column on the game, but Lewis
would have were he not engaged
elsewhere.

This is a Mickey Mantle diversion
that did not involve Lewis. Mickey
had 4 autographed baseballs to
sell and asked Carey where Ty Cobb
was from. Carey told him Royston
and drove Mickey the 60 some miles
to the Ty Cobb Museum. It being
deer season the museum was
deserted, but Mickey waited two
hours for patrons to arrive. When
they did not Carey drove Mickey to
a pool hall. There the thrilled
owner fired a pistol in the air to
get everyone's attention. Mickey
waved a $100 bill and announced,
"Drinks on the house!". It was
said to be the loudest Mickey
Mantle introduction ever. No word
on whether he sold the 4

baseballs. Instead of making money that day Mickey was possibly down $100.

Returning to Lewis centered content, Carey treated me to lunch at a favorite Greensboro lunch spot, Holcomb's Bar B Que. Lewis was a frequent patron, and until not too long ago a photo of him dining there adorned a wall. When we entered I got all nervous wanting to order exactly what Lewis ordered if anyone remembered what that was. Carey ended the suspense by asking for "two plates". I suspected those plates came with food on them, and I was quickly proven right.

But first, Holcomb's is now proudly operated by 2nd generation family owners. Though business thrives, no current owner remembers meeting Lewis. His photo no longer hangs on the wall. When Carey asked where that might be no one was really sure. I wanted to cry.

When the "plates" arrived I wanted to cry for a better reason. The food was exceptional, the presentation as plain as could be. Chopped pork, Brunswick Stew and cole slaw on a sectioned paper plate. Slices of white bread on the side, washed down with a Co-Cola. Carey had sweet tea. I still can't gag down tea of any variety. I would have licked my plate and Carey's too, but Carey introduced me to Kirby Smart's UGA roommate. He is an esteemed local official and was holding court at a nearby table. Were he to be a prospective future interview candidate a dual plate licking on my part may not be the best possible first impression.

I shall see Carey again soon. Lewis's favorite Swingin' Medallions will play Greene County

in a few weeks. I will attend and
perhaps cover the performance
freelance for the Greensboro
Herald Journal.

But first I gotta finish writing a
book.

Mark Reed, Shelton Stevens & Jerry Baker

Mark Reed is Lewis's fraternity brother who I found via a Google search long before I began to write this book. His blog referenced an Atlanta Swingin' Medallions band party where Lewis and Mark hijinks ensued. When I first reached Mark he insisted he did not know Lewis that well. He since told me he and Lewis met for a BBQ lunch, where Lewis speculated he did not expect to survive his 4th surgery. I have yet to meet Mark but suspect him to simply be a modest guy.

Mark was instrumental in introducing me to Shelton Stevens and Jerry Baker, two of Lewis's closest friends. Though I include chapters on each of them, here I include a "gift chapter" written by Mark and Shelton, shared with their permission. This is verbatim from an email. I only separated a few paragraphs.

Grizzard/Stevens/Baker Relationship

Shelton Stevens

to me

Peter, thought you'd enjoy this. Below is a Mark Reed "repost" of something I put up on Facebook a few years back, about the history of the relationship shared between three young Freshmen back in 1964:

Lewis Grizzard, Jerry Baker and myself. I think you'll agree that it was a memorable relationship that had its beginning during our undergraduate days, dating from 1964 - 1968. Some pretty remarkable "sports" things

happened during that time, that
will never happen again:

Dooley came in our freshman year
as Head Coach at UGA with some
unforgettable accomplishments
(Dodd's demise at GT, beat the
hell out of Spurrier/UF, went to
four bowl games, won 2 SEC
Championships, beat Bear Bryant,
etc.), 3 pro franchises came to
Atlanta (Hawks, Braves & Falcons),
etc. Bake and I had 10+ football
lettermen (most starters, some
All-SEC, some went on to NFL) as
our "Little Brothers" in the
fraternity. Also, had an All-SEC
basketballer (Dickie McIntosh) and
best pitcher on baseball team
(Mike Wysocki - SF Giants).

All this, while Grizzard was
laying the groundwork toward
becoming the "Southern
Institution" he grew to be in the
world of journalism.

Reed's Intro: The following is a comment made by fraternity brother Shelton Stevens about and to fraternity brother Jerry D. Baker about the two of them and fellow fraternity brother Lewis Grizzard...Shelton gave me permission to share it...it was a wonderful time...great memory...

Shelton's quote:

"Jerry Baker and Lewis Grizzard were two of my closest buddies ever. We found out our Freshman year that we had more in common than most and formed a friendship that lasted a lifetime. One from the inner city (Sylvan), one from the suburbs (Briarcliff), and one from a small, rural town (Moreland/Newnan HS) in west GA.

Three guys that bonded early on around PBRs and a love of sports at a time that no one will ever experience again in the state of

Georgia: 1) our beloved UGA catching up to and surpassing GT in football dominance and never looking back as young Vince Dooley forced the legendary Coach Dodd into early retirement after 4-straight losses. We beat The Bear on a Flea-Flicker, pounded Gator QB Steve Spurrier into a submission he never forgot, won two SEC Championships in three years and played in four bowl games (Sun, Liberty, Cotton & Sugar); 2) Professional sports coming to Atlanta: the Hawks (NBA), the Braves (MLB) and the Falcons (NFL); 3) The Masters a few miles away in Augusta with Arnie & the Bear at the beginning their run.

Between us, Bake and I proved to be two of the best recruiters in UGA history with "Little Brothers" on the football team including: Ronnie Jenkins, Ronnie Tidmore, Jimmy Layfield, Johnny Ingram,

David Rholetter, Ronnie Huggins, Mike Lopatka, Johnny Campbell, Barry Outlar, Jimmy Shirer. Throw in All-SEC basketballer, Dickie McIntosh, and pitcher, Mike Wysocki (SF Giants) - we pretty much had UGA athletics covered. Jerry married his college sweetheart, Joye. I married mine - Tena. Good ole Uncle Lew, bless his heart, married "many".

We ALL still attend and enjoy UGA football games together every Fall in Classic City - Bake and I in person, still enjoying the PBRs. Lewis sits between us - in spirit - keeping the beer cold and keeping us smiling . . . as only he could. God Bless and Go Dawgs!!!!"

Mark, Shelton and Jerry:

Thank you for the gift of this chapter!

Swingin' Medallions, Jerry & Joye Baker

In early January I was in Athens to meet Lewis contacts not yet determined. While trying to figure out who might be available I decided to research Lewis's favorite band, The Swingin' Medallions. I knew they still toured but did not know how often or where.

A glance at The Swingin' Medallions website revealed they were to perform at The Foundry in Athens on Saturday night, 48 hours after I thought of them. This is how things have been happening.

I commenced to doing several things. I first called Robby Cox, the Medallions contact. Turned out Robby had been the drummer for years and took time off touring to manage bookings from the comfort of his home. Robby confirmed the band was indeed playing Athens and put me in touch with Josh Snelling, who would be my on site contact.

I next reached out to Lewis's friends who I knew were Medallions enthusiasts. Several were in Atlanta, so their attendance on short notice was unlikely. But I did get confirmation from Jerry Baker that he and his wife would attend. Jerry was mentioned in several pages of conversation notes from Sigma Pis and others. I knew he was in the Athens vicinity, but Lewis's friends are always on the move. The call advising he could join me at The Medallions was perfect. I could check two boxes on my "to see" list. Plus folks who were likely more than a little fun would join me for the fun.

Robby Cox advised that a elder
Medallion Jimmy Perkins would be
the band member most likely with
Lewis memories to share. Over the
years there have been around 80
Medallions, many are the sons,
relatives or friends of the
originals. When we met Jimmy said
he remembered Lewis well but could
not think of a specific experience
all these years later.

A younger guy chimed in, "I got
some Lewis stories!' That guy was

Richard Loper, a Medallion from
1987 to 2002 who rejoined the
group in 2017. Richard's ex-
mother-in-law, Judith, is the 2nd
generation owner and publisher of
the Index-Journal newspaper in the
Medallions' home town of Greenwood
South Carolina. Judith's mother
previously owned the paper and
smoked a pipe. Pretty safe to
conclude there are characters in
Richard's ex-family. The Index-
Journal carried Lewis's column,
and Richard advised that his
Judith knew Lewis and had
remarkable stories to share. I
have yet to reach Judith.

Back to the Medallions shortly. Before the band got rocking Jerry "Bake" Baker found me. It took him a while in the crowd because I was not wearing the newspaperman Panama hat I told him to look for. My Momma told me gentlemen do not wear hats indoors, so I was hatless even though I was long ago evicted from the gentleman club.

Jerry introduced his lovely wife Joye, and we dove into conversation. I quickly learned Joye's younger brother is Jim Brady, a founding member of my own Phi Gamma Delta fraternity who now lives in Hawaii. I last saw Jim when I was about 11, and he was a riot. I am told he still is, albeit a far less preppy riot than he was in 1968. I would learn later that Jerry was an athletic UGA stud and Joye was a UGA cheerleader. Jerry did not use the word "stud". I apply that description, but only in a manly way.

The Bakers had heard the Medallions many times at many places over the years, including private parties where Lewis or Sigma Pis hired them around Atlanta for any occasion and Sea Island before Georgia Florida games.

During a break I met backstage with Richard Loper and heard fuzzy Lewis stories. Many are mentioned elsewhere in this book. I will digress into stories unrelated to Lewis. Long ago the Medallions headed west to play Vegas with Frank Sinatra. They blew a speaker in route and apologized to Frank upon arrival. Within 15 minutes not one but two brand new replacement speakers arrived. After the performance they asked Frank what to do with the speakers. His reply, "Oh those. They're yours."

Frank invited the Medallions out west for some more permanent arrangement. Members explained that they were also college students to both get an education and avoid Viet Nam. Frank said he could take care of the Vietnam part. The Medallions chose to remain in far less glitzy South Carolina.

The Swingin' Medallions have the unique distinction of having played with legends from Sinatra and his Rat Pack to Bruce Springsteen. The Foundry was jammed the night of their performance with patrons from age 20 to 80. Those I talked to who have heard them over the decades said the current band sounds better than ever.

At the end of the night Jerry and Joye invited me to join their Sunday school class the following morning at Athens First United Methodist Church. See chapter on Jerry Baker & Tommy Lyons.

On Sunday Jerry and Joye invited me to their home outside Athens. Like Vince and Barbara Dooley and Shelton Stevens, their house is a shrine to UGA, walls adorned with priceless memorabilia. Call for their address if you would like to burgle the place. I get half of all swag you can grab without getting shot.

Now, back to Lewis. Per the
chapter on Mark Reed, Shelton
Stevens & Jerry Baker, Shelton,
Jerry and Lewis were thick as
thieves from UGA days until Lewis
died. Many of their stories appear
elsewhere.

Jerry had these new ones to offer,
with colorful detail offered up by
Joye.

In a west central Georgia city of
30,000 the major industrial

employer hired Lewis to speak at their annual holiday banquet. At some point the very somber and sober chief executive brought over an 80 year old employee who always wished to hug Lewis Grizzard before she died. Lewis was not so somber or sober. When they reached him and asked for the lady's hug, Lewis was unable to stand at that particular moment. He was preoccupied with someone under the table in an activity I will leave to the reader's imagination.

Maybe that someone tied Lewis's shoelaces together. But Guccis don't have laces so that probably was not it.

Lewis once spoke at the Columbus Georgia UGA Touchdown Club. A leading retailer and major donor begged for Lewis to just drop by the retailer's house after the meeting. He asked, "Lew, will you just come hang out at my place for a few minutes?" Lewis reluctantly agreed to do so. With Jerry behind the wheel, when they got to the guy's house over 100 people were in the front yard. Word had leaked. Jerry drove Lewis to the back entrance. The two of them visited with the retailer in his kitchen while friends and neighbors awaited a Lewis appearance. This time Lewis did not oblige. After the "few minutes" Lewis agreed to he and Jerry snuck back out the back way and disappeared into the night.

One last point about Jerry. In high school and early UGA days he had a 30 inch waist and 50 inch chest, a factoid offered by Joye. In other words, Jerry was an anatomical freak of nature. Today he is somehow shrunken yet remarkably fit. Kinda like going from the Incredible Hulk to Don Knotts. This is not a slight to

Jerry, as both Hulk and Barney
were mighty handsome.

Jerry Baker & Tommy Lyons

I am running into unusual connections between Lewis's Sigma Pi fraternity and my Phi Gamma Delta fraternity. Phi Gamma Delta did not exist at UGA when Lewis was in school. Sigma Pi shrank considerably or temporarily did not exist when I was in school. Yet both boasted campus leaders in their time.

The Phi Gamma Delta president my freshman year was John "Chomper" Chambers, who after graduation was next door neighbor to Lewis Grizzard friend and fraternity brother Shelton Stevens. With Chomper as president our chapter won its second Cheney Cup, meaning we were the best Phi Gam Chapter on Planet Earth.

Today 1/6/19, I made a most remarkable new discovery by attending First United Methodist

Church of Athens Sunday school
with another of Lewis's Sigma Pi
brothers and early UGA roommate,
Jerry "Bake" Baker. Jerry and I
met by design for the first time
last night at a performance of the
Swingin' Medallions, Lewis's
favorite band.

Jerry introduced me to the Sunday
school packed room of about 80
folks age 60 and up as a guy
writing a biography of Lewis
Grizzard. Folks turned around to
look at us in the back row, a
section Jerry covets as being
reserved for hooligans. Jerry's
wife Joye sits far away among
respectable non hooligan females.

When Jerry announced that he and I
met at a Swingin' Medallions
performance folks perked up even
more. Many appeared remorseful
they did not know the group to be
in town. I proceeded to tell two
quick stories about (A) Lewis

preaching a mock sermon to his Callaway Gardens roommates complete with verbatim Bible verses spontaneously recalled and (B) a story familiar to some about the young, bicycle riding Baptist and Methodist preachers in his childhood home town of Moreland.

Those stories played well, I announced I could continue for an hour but won't and I sat down. The guy in front of me turned around and said, "I got a few Grizzard stories for you." I made a note of that, and we enjoyed a spirited discussion of the Epiphany.

When the session closed that guy joins Bake, Joye and me to share his story. First of all, he's not just a guy. He is Tommy Lyons MD, a legendary UGA center and guard who started 43 consecutive games over the course of six years with the Denver Broncos. Tommy did not tell me that. Bake filled me in a little, and I looked up the rest. Further, Tommy put himself through med school while playing in the NFL. Guy ain't no chump.

So, Tommy's story was about playing golf with Lewis at the Melrose Golf Club on Daufuskie Island near Savannah. Tommy owned a home there, and Lewis was a member with access to 'members in residence' cottages. Tommy got in the habit of looking to see if Lewis was in residence whenever Tommy was in residence.

One day circa 1985 Tommy, Lewis and 3rd golfer scheduled a round of skins, garbage, junk or trash. This is friendly wagering to those unfamiliar with such terms, kinda like me before this morning. Tommy had been stinking it up on the golf course for weeks and entered the competition with some trepidation. He admitted as much to Lewis, which only served to embolden Lewis.

Well, Tommy caught fire that day. After 9 holes it was Tommy 9, Lewis and golfer number 3 zero each. Lewis proposed to double the stakes. Others agreed. After holes 10 through 17 it was Tommy about 14-15, golfer number 3 about 2-3, Lewis zero. Lewis proposed to double the stakes again for hole 18. Others agreed. Golfer number 3 won that one, leaving Lewis completely skunked and with debt to the other two escalated only by his own doing.

Here's the remarkable part. Golfer number 3 was Tommy "TR" Rogers, president of UGA Phi Gamma Delta the year before I joined. TR as president earned the chapter our first Cheney Cup. What is it about Cheney Cup winning presidents later befriending friends of Lewis Grizzard?

Tommy Lyons is not a Sigma Pi. But Tommy is a friend of Jerry "Bake" Baker, who is a Sigma Pi. Thus, I make that another Phi Gam - Sigma Pi connection. Do not attempt to deter me from doing so.

To close this convoluted tale, Tommy Lyons MD is a gynecologist. Yet he saved Bake Baker during a Sunday school class when Bake collapsed with a severe case of vertigo. Gynecologists don't often save men's lives. Dr. Lyons asserted it was even more challenging with Bake being dead weight and the added difficulty of getting Bake's legs up in the stirrups.

I had planned to meet friends for Sunday breakfast, but the vision of what Dr. Lyons described put a damper on my appetite.

Lastly, I now gotta call TR Rogers to hear whatever stories he may have about Lewis. This work never ends.

Fraternity Life

Lewis Grizzard was a member of the Sigma Pi fraternity at the University of Georgia. I have met or spoken with several of Lewis's Sigma Pi brothers, and they each have rich stories to tell.

One such brother asks to remain anonymous in what I write. So for the purposes of this column I will not name any brothers. All fraternities maintain secrets, but who is a member is not usually one of them. Let's just maintain an aura of Greek mystery for this column.

Lewis was not all that active in Sigma Pi, because he was a very busy student. He wrote up to six columns a week for the Athens Daily News. He was also a member of the Gridiron Secret Society. What his membership demands were there I do not know, because it is secret. Lewis was also married at age 19. Combine all this with academics, and that does not leave a whole lot of time for fraternity life. Yet he left his mark on at least a few Sigma Pi brothers.

The Swingin' Medallions are a still thriving band Lewis first heard in 1965 at another fraternity house while strolling around campus with his father. His dad commented, "Marvelous music. Simply marvelous." Lewis agreed. He went on to label the Medallions as "THE PARTY BAND OF THE SOUTH", and that label stuck. Sigma Pi hired the Medallions to play at Georgia Florida weekend parties and more. They still perform across the country and beyond, on cruise ships, at gubernatorial inaugural balls and on television.

The Swingin' Medallions performed at one Atlanta area Sigma Pi party shortly after Lewis graduated.

Lewis and the brother who booked the band were on stage in their preppy attire rolling around in spilled beer and who knows what else demonstrating the Gator dance, which is performed lying down and flopping somewhat more like a fish than a reptile.

Lewis and the brother ...

"... both looked at each other and smiled, and then both looked up at the same time at his wife standing on the table above us, doing her best Whisky A Go Go dance moves in her lovely mini skirt. We were not trying to look up her dress, but it just happened to be that we had the perfect angle of view. Brothers and sisters, I must report that she was not wearing any under garments."

To which Lewis looked over at his brother, grinned, and remarked,

"Whut can I say?". Presumably they went back to their flopping.

Another Sigma Pi brother explains Lewis's underappreciated intellect. During their single days Lewis and this brother annually went on two vacations together, one to snow ski, the other to raft down some river. On one rafting trip Lewis read The Rise and Fall of the Third Reich while on the Colorado River.

I read that book long ago. It is 1,280 pages, it took me a month and I was not contending with Class 5 rapids. I was not dealing with Class anything rapids. I was on dry land and summer vacation. And I took speed reading in high school. Rafting the Colorado River takes 8 days, and there are significant distractions that get in the way of reading complicated text. Yet Lewis managed. He did not skim the book, he read it.

Each night Lewis and his fellow rafters discussed in depth the intricacies of Adolf Hitler and WW2. There were very likely adult beverages involved. I can not get confirmation that Lewis was a speed reader. I only assume he must have been.

That same Sigma Pi used to tailgate with Lewis at UGA football games in Athens. In 1977 Lewis proposed alternative travel from Atlanta to Athens via a bus from a suburban Marriott parking lot. Lewis's brother protested, claiming he liked tailgating just steps from Sanford Stadium. Lewis prevailed in the discussion.

Come game day Lewis and the brother arrive at the Marriott lot to find a blue bus and a bunch of fans dressed in blue. It was a Kentucky team bus. Lewis confessed to having not done his usually thorough research. Kentucky waxed Georgia that day 33-0.

Following the game, Lewis had been marginally overserved. On the bus ride home his brother had to restrain Lewis, lest he get in 'some trouble'. The next day Lewis entirely reversed the roles. His brother chose the wrong bus, and Lewis had to restrain the brother lest he get in 'some trouble' on the ride back to Atlanta. This was also the game at which England's Prince Charles visited and one of several at which James Brown performed during halftime.

More on Charles and James another time.

This last is an example of Lewis playing loose with facts. In his reporter days he took very few such liberties. When he transitioned to columnist he could and did write what he wanted. And the world loved it.

Which make pursuit of facts as they relate to Lewis Grizzard an 'adventure', even when you talk to the people who were there when the facts were factual.

There are a few Sigma Pis I have yet to contact. We shall see what Lewis adventures they hold in store.

Dave Lieber

Lewis Grizzard has been my writing hero since I first began reading newspaper content beyond the comics. For hundreds of thousands of readers, he brought a daily smile with their AM coffee or PM beverage of choice.

In 2011 one noted columnist said this to fellow members of the National Society of Newspaper Columnists:

Why papers are dying: Lewis Grizzard died first

I wholeheartedly concur with Dave Lieber. I disagree with Mr. Lieber on the minor issue of Erma Bombeck, who I also read daily. Lewis gets my vote as "the most popular American columnist of the last half of the 20th century."

The evening after our December 11, 2018 lunch, Jim Minter sent me this via email:

You might call your book The Legend(s) of Lewis Grizzard

(And the death of newspapers as we knew them.)

Jim was the Atlanta Journal editor who hired Lewis before graduation from UGA, and he hired him again at the Atlanta Constitution after Lewis's stint in Chicago. Jim is too modest to admit it, but other notable folks assert that Jim was Lewis's closest lifelong friend and greatest journalistic influence.

The late Furman Bisher wrote this 1994 headline upon Lewis's death:

Not as much fun without Grizzard

Furman's closing line to that column:

"How times have changed, and so will our lives without Lewis Grizzard."

Amen.

Since Lewis died I have found no compelling reason to read any major metropolitan newspaper.

To my delight, many local community newspapers still thrive with excellent writing. They include but are not limited to, The Forsyth County News, The Greensboro Herald Journal (both in Georgia) and the many Florida, Georgia and Carolina publications of Community Newspapers Inc. I write for one and aspire to write for others. But this is a subject for future discussion.

Some described Lewis as "The Mark Twain of the South". Lewis was not the anything of anywhere. He was a pure original.

Even northerners he disparaged as "Yankees" confess that Lewis introduced them to the southern way of life. This was the case if they moved south or never even lived below the Mason-Dixon line. They reveal that what is funny in Georgia is funny in far corners of the US.

Despite some detractors, Lewis appealed to readers across North

America. At his peak his column was syndicated in 450+ newspapers. He went on to greater fame as a talk show guest, stand up comedian, actor and recording artist. He even enjoyed success as a somewhat half-baked songwriter and vocalist.

Weeks ago I began to wonder what happened to Lewis Grizzard stuff. I did rapid and extensive research and am still doing it. Most of that stuff is in storage where no one but archivists can see it.

I asked myself if this would be true of Mark Twain. I asked the same to others who knew Lewis casually or intimately. All agreed it is time to resurrect Lewis's legacy and honor him as the man who entertained so many for so long.

Lewis Grizzard left us far too early. The biography I am writing

will be for readers who miss him
and others who perhaps have never
seen his work. And it will be for
my sons, Kevin and Ben. They
deserve to know Lewis.

Churches

I am traveling across Georgia
while writing a biography of Lewis
Grizzard. Last night I poked
around online to look for a church
to attend today, Sunday morning,
December 16. I even gave thought
to calling a friend of Lewis's in
the area to ask where he went. I
thought better of it, as I did not
even know if he goes to church,
and that is a rather personal
question to ask someone you met
only once.

I expected to go to a local
Presbyterian church, but I was
surprised and excited to discover
a branch of my hometown
nondenominational church in the
vicinity. It was a 30 minute
drive, but I needed the home
pastor's message. More often than
not, that is broadcast to
satellite churches unless there is

some special message for the local congregation.

I arrived 5 minutes late, as has been my unintentional habit for as long as I have gone to church. I can usually blame it on my sluggish teenage sons, but they are unfortunately not with me on this trip. I could blame Lucifer, Beelzebub or Old Scratch, but I don't think any of them influences me this morning. Thus, I blame scenic country roads. It sure wasn't my fault.

I took a seat in the front row far left because I could not see a thing upon entering the dark room. The congregation now meets in the local cinema while they built what will be an impressive church home down the road. In the next instant I see Lewis's friend walk by and climb the steps, this time aided by an usher's flashlight. I ask the usher if that was in fact the guy I think it was. It was. These things have been happening a lot lately. I move up to where the guy and his wife are seated, briefly say hi and grab a seat.

As almost always, the pastor delivers a message as if it was to me alone and no one else in the room. Absolutely incredible. I took action on that message right after the service, a story for another time.

As we walked out of the theater I ask Lewis's friend who at the church I might contact to learn what other members of the congregation may have known Lewis. As Lewis has been gone almost 25 years, his friend had to ponder. He introduced me to two volunteers who might help. One of them was a big Lewis fan, the other had not heard of Lewis but will look him up after today.

The fact that Mickey Mantle introduced Lewis to the area is what piqued the last guy's interest. With the subject of Lewis Grizzard, it is real easy to think of a hook to pique virtually anyone's interest.

I left with a church email address and the names of folks to contact. I will not only inquire about Lewis contacts but also if the church may wish for me to come talk to a group about my book. Lewis told family friendly stories about churches and ministers - even to church groups. There is no reason I can not manage the same. For those in the know, one of several punch lines is, "Dang brother. I don't believe I'd a told that."

Lewis's jokes revolved primarily around Methodists, Baptists and TV evangelists. In his hometown of Moreland they occasionally encountered Presbyterians but ran them out of town. On this particular day I am glad I did not opt for the Presbyterian church as originally planned.

Maybe if I come back this nondenominational congregation will not run me out of town.

Perhaps a good place for a photo of Lewis's Moreland United Methodist Church:

Frederick Allen

Every Lewis Grizzard friend I talk to refers me to at least one other person to talk to, usually several. Occasionally I stumble upon an excellent source on my own. Such is the case with Frederick Allen, who I just learned goes by Rick.

After graduation from UGA I lived in Atlanta from 1980 to 1983, whereupon I moved to Chicago. I read Rick's column regularly. It was not satire, it was business and just great writing. Late last week I discovered that Lewis once resigned or threatened to resign from the Atlanta Constitution over two issues. They fired Ron Hudspeth, and they let Frederick Allen 'get away'.

I thought it would be good to reach Mr. Allen, and I was correct. Before our talk moments ago I researched to find that he wrote Secret Formula, *the* definitive history of the Coca-Cola Company, and Atlanta Rising, one of a few definitive histories of Atlanta. I now have two more books I must read when I stop writing.

I reached out to Rick via Emory University, and he graciously and promptly called me back. My dad was a career Coke guy, so Rick and I swapped a bunch of stuff on that topic. In a way his multi-year effort to write 'Formula' parallels what will hopefully be my months long effort to write 'Grizzard".

Rick started by researching and writing about Robert Woodruff, and he found hundreds of unindexed boxes of papers at Emory. I started by just looking for Lewis stuff, and I found 19 well indexed boxes of papers at the University of Georgia. Rick's project grew from Woodruff to the entire Coca-Cola Company. My project will absolutely not grow from Lewis to the entire Atlanta Journal-Constitution.

Rick got a big name publisher real quick. I hope to get a publisher big or small, but it ain't happening quick. Rick started as a somebody. I started and continue as a nobody. Except maybe to my sons and people to whom I owe money.

Rick and Lewis did not have warm early relations. They did not necessarily have cold early relations. They were simply two talented writers writing very different content at the same paper. Rick wrote serious stuff, and Lewis wrote Lewis. Rick's column and Lewis's ran on alternating days. Rick appreciated that Lewis brought him thousands of readers. They might go looking for Lewis and find Rick. They would read his column and tell themselves that Frederick guy sure can write. I was one of those readers looking for Lewis but happy to find Rick.

Rick and Lewis warmed to each other considerably at the 1980 Democratic National Convention in New York. Jimmy Carter was re-nominated, so Atlanta media got very good seats. Willie Nelson came out to sing the National Anthem. He had a bottle of whiskey in one hand and a blonde on the arm not attached to any bottle. Willie could not remember many of the lyrics to the Star Spangled Banner. Perhaps that was the night Lewis became a major Willie Nelson fan. Because of the blonde and bottle, not because he forgot much of the Anthem.

That night Rick and Lewis went out on the town. Others may have joined them to start, but the two of them outlasted the rest. What pub they went to Rick does not recall. It may have been several. Adult beverages got consumed in considerable volume, and Rick and Lewis became friends. This is not the first time I have heard that Lewis warmed to someone after moderate to extensive lubrication, and it will not be the last.

Regarding Rick's 1987 departure from the Atlanta paper, he says, "I felt like I got shot by the cavalry during a rescue." He left on his own terms to join CNN, yet the firestorm in his wake blazed on. Lewis obviously stayed at or returned to the paper.

In Atlanta Rick and Lewis did not frequent the same after hours media haunts. Rick was a Mr. C's guy, Lewis a Harrison's (and others) guy. I have yet to find a Manuel's guy in all this research, though I believe that will come in time. Lewis was known to stray.

For now I must add Rick's Secret Formula and Atlanta Rising to my Christmas list. Or to my shopping list if two disobedient sons already bought me socks or a tie. I've told my boys that if it was good enough for Lewis to shun socks and ties it is good enough for me.

But sometimes teenagers just don't listen.

Mr. Anonymous

One of Lewis's friends with whom I spoke prefers to fly under the radar, as he did with pleasure when Lewis wrote about him. This guy was Lewis's buddy when they were both single. It went kinda like this.

The name referenced below is fictitious to protect the guilty and innocent.

Lewis wrote about this guy using his Christian and legal first name because he thought it sounded more southern than what the guy was known as his entire life. Plus, he did not think the name by which the guy was known was funny enough.

Thus, we discuss the Lewis Grizzard experiences with one Rooster Skid Marks. While everyone knew him as Skid Marks, Lewis wrote about him as Rooster Marks. So no one ever knew who the guy Lewis was writing about really was. Do you follow?

Rooster Marks and Lewis went on two annual bachelor trips for a few years. In the winter they would ski, never at the same resort twice. In the summer they would raft, never down the same river twice.

Rooster observed to me that Lewis had an intellect few among the general public understood. Case in point, by far their most adventurous rafting trip was on the Colorado River. On that trip Lewis read The Rise and Fall of the Third Reich. Last I checked that book was 1,245 pages. Lewis didn't skim it. He read it. I once read it, and it took me something like 6 weeks. Rooster did not specify the duration of their trip, but the longest I can find lasts 8 days. Rooster did not specify if Lewis read while his raft careened down Class 5 rapids or only during more tranquil spans of the river. Rooster did specify that each evening Lewis held sway over the rafting party discussing in intricate detail WW2 and the politics of Nazi Germany.

I have found no one to confirm it, yet this leads me to believe that Lewis was, among so many other things, a speed reader. Maybe he even had a photographic memory. It is too bad Lewis did not sit still long enough and/or was not curious and/or introspective enough to get tested for such qualities.

Rooster and Lewis used to tailgate together at Georgia football games, home and away. The week before the 1977 home game against Kentucky Lewis called Rooster with a brilliant idea. "Let's take a

shuttle bus from Atlanta to
Sanford."

Rooster argued against it, as they
tailgated only steps from the
stadium. Taking a shuttle would
mean leaving both Atlanta and
Athens earlier, traveling with
strangers, losing control of their
itinerary and very likely having
to walk further to and from
Sanford.

Lewis argued, "But we can drink
more."

Rooster continued to resist, but
Lewis prevailed.

Arriving at the suburban Atlanta
hotel parking lot Lewis and
Rooster noticed something neither
expected. People waiting around
for the bus to arrive were all
dressed in blue, not UGA red and
black. Lewis had scheduled them on
a Kentucky fan bus.

Rooster commented that Lewis could and should have researched this boondoggle a little better, but by then they had few alternatives. They had given their tailgate spot to friends and had already consumed a number of adult beverages at breakfast.

Aside from some good natured banter with Wildcat fans the ride to Athens was uneventful. The game was anything but uneventful. James Brown performed at halftime, England's Prince Charles attended - probably thinking it was a soccer match. Fans unfurled a banner from the bridge that read "Prince Charles Does it Doggy Style", and Kentucky waxed the Dawgs 33-0. Lewis and Rooster loitered with their tailgate friends and consumed a significantly higher number of adult beverages to justify their having opted not to drive themselves home. Then it was time to catch the bus.

The Kentucky bus.

Departure from Athens was uneventful for only the few minutes it took the bus to get from Sanford to The Varsity. Lewis politely requested that the driver stop at The V to allow Rooster, the assorted Wildcats and Lewis to sample Varsity cuisine. And to take a pee. The driver declined, rather rudely. Lewis was not accustomed to drivers who did not honor his polite requests, especially rude drivers wearing an opposing team's colors. Perhaps Lewis began that instant to think of Kentuckians and Yankees.

With that inauspicious start, the ride to Atlanta went downhill fast. Lewis was in a foul mood, and he aired his displeasure to the many otherwise reasonably well behaved victorious Wildcats, who significantly outnumbered Rooster and Lewis. Those Wildcats understandably took exception to Lewis's sharp tongue. They went from well behaved to telling Rooster they would kick Lewis's ass if Rooster did not shut Lewis's smart yap. After all, they were the victors. And the majority.

Rooster somehow managed to sufficiently contain overserved Lewis's yap, at least to the point that Wildcats refrained from kicking his ass for the hour plus ride back to the suburban Atlanta hotel parking lot. Rooster saw to it that Lewis arrived safely home.

In his column about the game Lewis reversed the roles 180 degrees. Rooster Marks was the guy who poorly researched the shuttle bus. Rooster Marks was overserved and belligerent to the point that

Lewis had to heroically step in and prevent a horde of Wildcats from seriously kicking some Rooster ass.

Such is the luxury of Lewis the columnist. He had no obligation to strictly adhere to facts. His column indeed cited many facts accurately, just not strictly.

Had I Lewis's powers of metaphor I would close this tidily by abstractly associating WW2 experiences in the book Lewis read on the Colorado River with Kentucky Wildcat fan behavior on that bus ride home. But today's hypersensitive political correctness does not reward writers for associating any group with WW2 Germans, so I will refrain.

Plus, unlike Lewis, I am a chicken.

The Four Wives of Lewis II

Technically, that should read "The Four Wives of Lewis, Jr.", but let's stick with what is up there.

What is up there has the ring to it of "The Six Wives of Henry VIII", which is a pretty popular story.

Like Lewis Grizzard II, Henry Tudor VIII was a complicated guy. Henry VIII also complicated a lot of things around him, including the lives of his six wives. He complicated at least two of those six wives' lives to the extent that he ended those lives by separating the wives' heads from their bodies.

This was all due to the wives' inability to give Henry a male heir. We now know that the male is genetically responsible for the gender of offspring, but Henry would not likely have let that detail get in the way had he known it. Henry was a headstrong guy who did not want to be confused with facts.

Lewis did not produce an heir, male or female. The reasons for this may come to light later, but history does not tell us he executed any of his wives because of it. Witnesses tell me that all four of Lewis's wives attended his memorial and perhaps even sat together. They could not have done that had one or more of them been executed.

You see, I am trying to write a fun book about Lewis, and I already veered off course and started talking about gruesome execution and decapitation. I will aspire to do that as infrequently as possible.

Back to Henry complicating things. He complicated things at church, as in he started a new one. The Catholic church was pretty much the only Christian church on the planet when Henry was born. When the Catholic church would not allow Henry to divorce, he started his own church, the Church of England. It was a lot like the Catholic church, except Henry was the head of it instead of a pope, and it allowed at least Henry to get a divorce.

Pretty cool to make a new church overnight, become the leader of it, and tell everyone who reports to you they now belong to the church where you are the boss. That would eventually lead to Pilgrims and Puritans and a place called America, but not for another century.

Lewis also had a complicated relationship with church that he talked about a lot. It primarily involved the Methodist faith to which he belonged and the Baptist faith to which he did not. These existed long before Lewis was born, and they got started for some of the same reasons that led to the Puritans.

Lewis was certainly not a Puritan, yet history does not reveal that he ever tried to invent a new church with himself at the top of it.

Lewis did not like many TV evangelists, particularly those who would sweat and cry right after getting caught committing adultery in some cheap hotel room despite raking in millions of dollars each week. Had TV existed, Henry would likely have taken to the airwaves on BBC, a network he would have naturally owned, to promote his terrific new Church of England. Henry was rather chunky, and AC was not yet invented, so he too would have probably sweat a lot in front of the camera.

But Henry probably would not have cried or gotten caught committing adultery in some cheap hotel room. He owned all of the nice hotels in England, and no one would likely betray his adultery, because every hotel probably had a guillotine suite, which he also owned.

I know, the guillotine was French and not yet invented when Henry was ordering heads to be severed. He did not allow facts to get in his way, nor did Lewis. Nor do I.

Sorry, there I go typing gruesome stuff again. Dang it.

In case you are wondering what my point is, I will attempt to return to it here and now.

Despite recommendations by several of Lewis's high level friends that I do so, I do not plan to interview Lewis's ex-wives for this book. They now lead private lives, and I wish them well. Though they may be able to reveal why Lewis fathered no children - or heirs - I do not wish to go into Lewis's bedroom, historically, figuratively or literally.

If the wives themselves wish to unite to write a book, or if some other writer wishes to interview them and write a book about their lives with Lewis, that will be great by me. They can use the title of this column if they wish. I make no claim to it.

It might even sell a few books to overserved readers who think they are buying The Six Wives of Henry VIII.

Bill Oberst Jr.

Bill Oberst Jr. toured portraying Lewis Grizzard on stage for over a decade and still makes occasional encore appearances in the role. He established a niche in one man acts and has performed in virtually every acting medium. He has the likely unique distinction of being the only human to play Mark Twain, Adolf Eichmann, William Tecumseh Sherman, John F. Kennedy, Abraham Lincoln and Jesus of Nazareth.

Among many awards over his illustrious career, Bill was recipient of the first Lon Chaney Award For Outstanding Achievement In Independent Horror Films in 2014.

IMDb describes him cast as "macabre, menacing characters with an undercurrent of melancholy".

Mr. Oberst's email to me:

Peter,

I'm gratified to read that you are considering a Grizzard bio. Yes, I'd be pleased to provide any information that might be helpful. Please feel free to send me any questions, and don't worry about taking up my time. I owe much to the experience of portraying him; it would be a small enough payment on that large debt to aid in any serious attempt to examine his life and significance.

Playing dead people has been a fascinating occupation. Memories fade, fame recedes and the quiet of the grave closes, eventually, over all. When I began playing Grizzard, his grave was almost always adorned with remembrances when I'd stop by on road tours of

the show. Now it is barren.
Sometimes, after a performance in
some small Southern community, an
older woman would grab my hand in
both of hers and say, quietly,
"Lewis was a good boy. We sure did
love him." I wondered who else she
was thinking of in that moment.

Forgive my waxing poetic - I'm
deep into my Ray Bradbury script
today, and the mind wanders.

With best regards,

Bill

Bill will soon tour the US
portraying Ray Bradbury. When he
comes my way I hope to shake his
hand.

Bobby Poss

I have always wanted to meet an Athens Poss, and I still do. During my college years I attended events at their vast Poss's Lakeview facility and ate "pig sandwiches" at their restaurant. I bought their canned Brunswick Stew at grocery stores and enjoyed what was for years the only imaginative Sanford Stadium concession stand offering - more Poss's pig sandwiches. Only Sanford simply labeled them as "BBQ Sandwich".

While writing this book I stayed at "a Poss home" owned by a friend of a friend. My hostess was a retiree from the West Coast who knew little about her house and unfortunately cared zero about college football. But she is a hoot with family members on UGA staff, so I overlooked her absence of Dawgs gridiron passion.

Without giving away too much about
the place, it is architecturally
significant and in a highly
desirable close in Athens
neighborhood abundant with green
space and wildlife. My hostess
knew only that it was once owned
by Posses. I informed her Poss is
a legendary Athens name, but the
Poss food company was no longer in
business for reasons I could not
recall. The phone book revealed
many Posses still in the area. I
offered to put my real estate
research experience to work on my

hostess's behalf to determine which Poss owner the house. I was a lot more interested than my hostess.

Later, when flying through the highly entertaining 2007 read, <u>The Naked Lady of Lake Oconee</u>, given to me by the author, I again stumbled upon the Poss name. Bobby Poss. Though author Carey Williams claimed the book to be entirely fictitious, he used certain names of real people to give those people thanks, recognition or simply a chuckle. I do not know how Bobby Poss fit into that equation, but I figured Carey could put me in touch with Bobby. Indeed Carey could, but Bobby was not around Lake Oconee, he was back in Athens. Trying to chase Lewis Grizzard people was getting to be like chasing wet cats around a countryside full of rodents.

In case you were wondering what all this had to do with Lewis, I am getting to that. Like right now.

First of all, Bobby Poss could be called Mr. UGA, Mr. Athens, Mr. No Longer Allowed to Speak at Touchdown Club Meetings Due to Political Incorrectness and many other titles. Bobby Poss is also a very funny man.

Second, Bobby seems to know everyone in America, much less almost everyone mentioned in this book. And Bobby knew Lewis Grizzard well.

Third, Bobby grew up in the Athens house where I wrote much of this book. That place is not "a Poss house". For many years it was "the main Poss house" and site of extravagant entertainment. Though Bobby could not recall if Lewis slept there, even for a catnap, he certainly partied there. What are the stinkin chances?!

At age 70 Bobby still works as 'salesman' for the adult beverage distributor founded by the late UGA Heisman Trophy winner Frank Sinkwich. When Bobby and I exchanged voice messages trying to line up our initial call he was busily running around delivering holiday week hospitality packages to loyal Athens customers. Had I been in the Athens area at the time I would have paid Bobby to let me ride shotgun in his delivery vehicle. From that experience I might have been able to write 7 or 8 more books had I survived the laughter.

I still have Bobby's most entertaining first voice message and would share it if it did not reveal confidential phone numbers. In it he misquoted Lewis as having coined 'GATA', as in "get after their ass". That was Erk Russell, but now is not the time to split hairs with a 70 year old adult beverage delivery man.

Bobby and I scheduled a Saturday call on December 22 while he would be in his office furiously working on holiday business without anyone else around making disturbing noises. I enjoyed the luxury of a similar distraction free environment during our call. That was a good thing, as it was as wild a ride as I might have sitting shotgun in his delivery vehicle.

Bobby was a center and long snapper on the UGA football team from 1968 to 1971. I seem to bond well with centers, especially those who snapped better than me, which is the entire population of centers on earth.

Bobby is a rare Bulldog athlete, born and raised in Athens and who never left. After a knee injury doomed his sophomore season he claims to be the only player Vince Dooley ever "called out of retirement."

His family moved into the Athens house where I stay when Bobby was 11. They moved the hedges that still line the driveway from his grandparent's house. He can tell the new owner when they glassed in a screen porch, added other screen porches and built the mammoth freestanding backyard BBQ pit. That is if I can ever get Bobby to his old house to meet the new owner. They both move around way too fast and often for people who are retired or should be.

At that party house they hosted innumerable poker games, football weekend parties and corporate hospitality events. Senior execs

from Winn Dixie would lodge on one
floor with execs from competing
Colonial Foods on the other floor,
all getting along famously for the
duration of their stays. Gawd
knows who has slept in the
smallest bedroom with two twins I
occupy, occasionally with one of
my sons in tow. If I can ever meet
Bobby there and he can remember
anything I will be delighted to
find out. Until he convinces me
otherwise I assert that Lewis or
his date slept in the bed I use.
Except they are new beds, and
Lewis did not likely seek twin
bedrooms with dates. Do not
confuse me with facts.

Too many stories get blurred.
Lewis's Athens Daily News cohort
Chuck Perry was a friend and
frequent visitor at the Posses. If
I ever complete this chapter the
next one I write will be on Chuck,
who minutes ago sent an email
clarifying Lewis's years in

Chicago at the behest of Jim Minter. Some encyclopedia website had Lewis in Chicago for almost 7 years, whereas I correctly had him there for under 3 years. So much for the sanctity and fact chucking truthiness of encyclopedias.

Bobby advised that his brother-in-law Mike Williams owned another Athens landmark frequented by Lewis and me, Charlie Williams Pinecrest Lodge. To my knowledge Lewis and I were never there on the same occasion. Mike sadly passed away in 2018. He would have had yet more Lewis stories to tell.

I was always curious about the demise of Poss's food empire. After Poss's Lakeview closed Castleberry Foods bought the canning plant but kept the Poss brand alive. Bumble Bee Foods then bought Castleberry and ultimately killed the Poss brand due to product duplication or some such. If someone can tell me where to buy a can of Bumble Bee Brunswick Stew I am all ears. If tuna is now an ingredient I will sue Bumble Bee for violating Brunswick Stew etiquette. That would be a far worse offense than Lewis's cardinal sin of calling beef BBQ.

Bobby Poss first got to know Lewis at the Athens Daily News when Bobby was a star on the Athens High football team. Lewis's first gig was covering high school sports, reporting to Wade Saye and working with Chuck Perry. Again, see separate chapters on Wade and Chuck. Bobby Poss Sr. was a big supporter of Vince Dooley, as was Lewis. Lewis therefore took special interest in anyone with the last name of Poss.

Over the years the Posses were involved with golf tournaments at Sky Valley, Lake Rabun, Clayton's

Kingwood Country Club and Kenny Rogers's Beaver Dam Farms in Colbert. Legends from the world of sports, music, broadcasting and general industry traveled from all around the globe to attend events, each replete with a combination of gambling, adult beverages and wee hour shenanigans. Do you see a familiar pattern here?

At the much ballyhooed pre Georgia Florida game Gator Hater tournaments Lewis and Bobby would alternate telling stories. That likely happened at other tournaments too, though Bobby talked too fast, and I don't take shorthand.

Lewis and Bobby might even get into a back and forth exchange, one trying to out story the other. Believe it or not, the interplay might result in something marginally off color, such as:

Bobby: If I come to your house and get your wife pregnant we'd be kin.

Lewis: No, we'd be even.

I had to think on that one for a minute. But Bobby was off on another tangent so I just tried to keep up.

Another Lewis and Bobby commonality is political incorrectness. Bobby was once a frequent speaker at UGA's Touchdown Club banquets. Despite his best efforts to tone down rhetoric as requested, Bobby is far less often invited to take the podium than he once was. He adapts to the reduction in visibility by telling stories before or after meetings when no one monitors conversation. Sounds like a Lewis solution to me.

Bobby and Lewis also shared heart issues albeit at very different stages of their lives. Most recently Bobby died in 2016 while riding his bike. As in dead as a doornail dead. Paramedics arrived quickly, packed him in ice and miraculously revived him. Like Lewis, Bobby attests that when doctors tell you something is not going to hurt they are lying like hell. If they tell you "This might burn a little." it will feel "like a flame thrower up your ass". Sorry children. Bobby has a mild case of potty mouth that my typing fingers can not bring themselves to cleanse.

Bobby otherwise told stories of UGA athletes who got their first jobs at Poss's Food's, paid to do nothing more than throw footballs or otherwise hone skills that would enable them to help defeat opponents. Many of those went on to be most charitable individuals themselves. One was charitable on many levels but not so much when it came to University of Georgia Athletic Administration requests. That person charged $100 to write a recruitment letter to coveted high school athletes. He had such big name cachet that the university reluctantly agreed to pay it. For obvious reasons I do not divulge the names of such individuals.

Nancy Hanson

Many have told me I need to talk to Ludlow Porch. I would love to, as he was yet another favorite in my childhood household. What I knew and some others unfortunately did not is Ludlow passed away in 2011.

Ludlow's Christian name was Bobby C. Hanson, and he was Lewis's step-brother. Ludlow was 12 years older than Lewis. Lewis's Dad very briefly married Ludlow's mother. Lewis and Ludlow never lived in the same house, but they became close friends. Ludlow was a Marine and served in the Korean War, as did Lewis's father in the Army. That may have made for interesting dynamics.

Ludlow was a radio fixture in the home of my youth as the soft spoken gentle humorist on Atlanta's pioneering talk station,

WRNG radio. People just called it "Ring".

Ludlow had regular callers he referred to as Whackos, and you could listen to their inanely hilarious banter for hours. Or maybe it was hilariously inane banter.

Jim Minter is a rare guy who is up to speed on a lot of things, and he referred me to Ludlow's widow, Nancy Hanson. Among other noteworthy achievements, Jim told me Nancy won a competition to write the lyrics for University of North Georgia's alma mater. With that introduction Nancy and I agreed to a phone call on December 23.

One item of great concern before we spoke was Nancy's email recommendation to read Ludlow's book, <u>Lewis and Me and Skipper Makes Three</u>. I had a ton of book reading to do but not until I finished this one. Yet that did not prevent me from doing quick research on such books. To the volume Nancy named I added Ludlow's Fat White Guys Cookbook and Who Cares About Apathy.

Of the volume Nancy recommended goodreads.com said:

"Porch and Grizzard (Jr.), two of the South's funniest funnymen, happen also to be step-brothers, so who better than Porch to reveal all the tales Grizzard never told on himself."

Well then. That would render my two months worth of work pointless. Yet upon closer look Ludlow's book was only 153 pages, and I had enough notes to maybe write 153 billion pages. I tried to stop hyperventilating.

Once composed I called Nancy and dove into a most enjoyable exchange. Ludlow did not marry no chump.

Nancy never met Lewis. She and Ludlow began dating in 1995, shortly after Lewis passed away and Ludlow's wife Diane passed away. Yet Nancy had plenty of 2nd hand Lewis stories to share, though they came to her first hand from a masterful teller of stories.

Nancy and Ludlow's late wife Diane were good friends. When Ludlow found himself single and lonely he turned to Nancy for companionship. He did not mince words and asked Nancy out on a date. He perhaps admired Nancy even more when she did not mince words in her reply.

"I will consider this under three conditions:"

1. I will never date a man who smokes.
2. I will never move with my until my son finishes school.
3. If you are anything like Lewis we are done.

Nancy did not say this, but I envision one spellbound and immediately smitten Ludlow.

1. He put out his cigarette and never lit up again.

2. He endured a grueling daily
   commute for months.
3. Re being anything like Lewis,
   Ludlow replied:

"You'll just have to determine
that for yourself."

Ludlow was as funny as Lewis, but
virtually all similarities between
the two ended there. Though
devoted to work, Ludlow
immediately became equally devoted
to Nancy. He commuted from Suwanee
to Fayetteville to Dawsonville
like a banshee during years when
Georgia Highway 400 was sheer
gridlock. Even today those are
hardly treks for the weary.

My first question to Nancy was
about Lewis's trip to the Soviet
Union. Jim Minter said he thought
it was some UGA related junket,
and he thought Lewis traveled
there with Ludlow. Jim was
correct.

Ludlow took Diane to Russia, and to Nancy's knowledge Lewis traveled solo. Aside from Ludlow recalling that their hotel rooms were bugged Nancy recalls few details. Bugged USSR hotel rooms in the 1990s would hardly come as a surprise, but I can only imagine what Lewis might have written about it or what Ludlow might have said about it. Yet I have thus far found nothing.

Lewis fell ill on the trip, and Ludlow insisted that Lewis depart immediately for treatment back home. Lewis was uncharacteristically obedient and followed his wise step-brother's advice. In London they wanted to hold Lewis for a month of antibiotics. There Lewis was disobedient and insisted on continuing to the States. Jim Minter met Lewis at the airport and delivered him to the hospital

- for a month of antibiotics. Lewis's neglected wisdom teeth became infected, and the infection went to his already frail heart. Read more about that in the chapter on Dr. Randy Martin.

I hoped that Nancy might be able to lead me to Grizzard first cousins, but she could not. Lewis's father was the youngest of 12 brothers and sisters. Ludlow may have been in touch with his step-cousins. If so, Nancy knew little if anything about them. As time wore on I increasingly believed that search to be in vain.

Nancy concluded that Ludlow said he was "hand holding in love" with her. She said in Ludlow's opinion Lewis was particularly "hand holding in love" with only one of his wives. In keeping with ex-wife neutrality, I shall not attach a name or even a number to that person. One would suspect they know who they are if it even matters any longer.

H. Richard Smith &
Sara Jane Skinner

Please pardon if elsewhere I spell
it as Sarah. That is how Lewis
spelled it. Then I found a Newnan-
Times Herald article spelling it
without the 'h'. Since that paper
is edited by her son Winton I
figure the paper got it right. I
have met with both mother and son,
yet we discussed just about
everything other than spelling.

The "Early Influences" chapter was
based on phone calls before
meeting the two after which this
chapter is named. The meeting was
almost as fun to schedule as it
was to attend. My early goal was
to get the two together with Jim
Minter. You know, early influences
with late influence would be a
blast. Due to holiday conflicts
that did not work out.

Yes, it should be the lady before the gentleman. But Richard taught Lewis in 10th grade, and Sara taught Lewis in 11th grade. Way back when I spoke to Richard on the phone before I spoke to Sara on the phone. And this ain't no tea dance, so get over it.

Richard and Sara(h) Jane were Lewis's high school English and journalism teachers, respectively.

I got Sara Jane to agree to a meeting first. I then called

Richard and suggested options before or after my meeting with Sara. Richard had much going on, so he had to kick around what might work with his calendar. He finally suggested that his driver/sister bring him to Sara's house and we all meet together. Hot dang! That is what I wanted to begin with. Sometimes if you keep your mouth shut long enough you get your wish.

On January 9 we met in the living room of Sara's lovely antebellum colonial. When I later asked the age, she referred to the best records they have. Per the 1830 census, no house. Per the 1850 census, house. She pointed out what was the original house and "new" circa 1870 addition. In other words, it is both antebellum and 'bellum'. I asked the original lot size. 202.5 acres. Not 200, 202, 203 or 205. 202.5 acres.

Christmas decorations were just coming down with ornament boxes scattered throughout. What I would give to have seen it in full holiday splendor.

Back to Sara and Richard. Once we were seated I quickly caught them up on what I knew from our phone conversations weeks prior. Sara was primarily an English teacher, but for her students to submit a Tiger Tracks section, the Newnan-Times Herald required that they teach a journalism class. Sara sought out the best available high school level journalism textbook. It was about the only available high school level journalism textbook. To teach that class Sara read a chapter the night before she taught that chapter. Lewis was in her class, in case you were wondering.

Some 15 years ago Richard was in the high school textbook storage room. He looked down and was surprised to see a copy of that very textbook on the floor. He was even more surprised to open it and find "Lewis Grizzard" in unmistakable handwriting. Lewis was the last owner of the book. Richard either stole the book or paid 5 cents. When I asked which, Sara chimed in, "Richard *earned* that book." And here I thought they might fight over it, or at least I was hoping.

To my dismay Richard loaned out the textbook for some Lewis commemorative event and has yet to get it back. I did my duty and got Richard and Sara all worried that someone might steal it. They now aspire to get it back.

Then I opened it up to the floor. Magic followed.

Sara and Richard go way back to before their teaching days

together. One of their relatives married a relative of the other. When Sara was a student teacher Richard was her student. When Sara became a full fledged teacher Richard became her student teacher. Then they taught together for a few decades. Unfortunately they had little more to say than that.

Okay, that was a lie.

Sara grew up just across the neighboring county line and went to a grade school worse than nearby Moreland Elementary in Coweta County. Her parent's property was in both counties, and they paid taxes in both counties. Though Sara could walk to the Coweta County line, her father paid tuition for her to attend the very good Newnan High.

I asked if Sara was a member of Moreland's Baptist or Methodist

church, as there is famously only
two to choose from. Well, that was
a little complicated and
scandalous. Her mother was a
Luthersville Presbyterian. The
infamy. Her father was a Moreland
Baptist deacon. When they married
after generations of devotion to
opposing denominations tongues
wagged to some degree. I thought
Lewis said Morelanders ran
Presbyterians out of town, but
Sara's mom obviously got a pass by
pretending to be Baptist the rest
of her life.

Richard grew up Methodist in
Moreland with no complications
relating to either scandalous
marriages or paid tuition at
public schools.

Sara grew up with coal and wood
stoves and heaters. Richard had an
early gas stove and heater.
Neither sickened or killed any

member of his family, so they must have been safe.

Lewis called Sara "Gypsy Woman" because she was attractive, olive complected and liked to wear purple. Lewis called Richard "Big Rich" because he was six foot two inches and weighed 120 pounds. Lewis was well behaved but very likely smitten by Gypsy Woman. He greatly admired Big Rich, but not necessarily smitten.

Lewis's first wife, then simply his friend, was also in Sara's journalism class. This may explain why Lewis was well behaved and did not act on his smittenness.

Richard played piano at Lewis's first wedding at Moreland Methodist. That was after high school, though not by much.

Back to high school days. Lewis was an early slave to fashion. He rarely wore socks with his penny loafers. This was long before he discovered or could afford Guccis. He would drag Dudley Stamps and Billy Thompson with him to check out the latest styles at Certean Cole men's clothing store. I hope I spelled that right. Everyone just called it 'The Store', perhaps because few could pronounce Certean.

After school those boys and others often bought a bottle of Coke and bag of peanuts. Lewis liked to dunk peanuts in Coke or drop them in the bottle. He claimed, "That is all the nutrition a man needs."

Once he hit the big time Lewis annually returned to stay at his childhood home with his mother over Thanksgiving. Each Wednesday night he would visit Scott's book store in Newnan to sign his latest book for customers. Scott's was a beloved institution if their 2013 still active Facebook page is any indication. It was run by Dick and Earlene Scott. Dick passed away in 2005, and Earlene carried on until she retired in 2013. I assume this is Earlene, and I hope sharing this photo is not a copyright violation.

When I first spoke by phone to Sara I did not realize Lewis's Wednesday night appearances before

Thanksgiving were an annual ritual. Nor did I realize Sara's appearances at what she hoped was the back of the book signing line was an annual ritual. She tried to not make anyone else wait, as she knew Lewis would make a fuss when she appeared. Inevitably a few stragglers would arrive late and get stuck during that fuss, but no one seemed to mind.

At the very last Wednesday Lewis made the biggest fuss of all. He hugged Sara, pulled up another chair and made her take a seat. He said next time he was in town he was going to come to her house, visit with her in rocking chairs on the porch and spit tobacco over the railing. Sara said Lewis never chewed that she knew of. "It was probably just the most disgusting thing he could think of to do on my front porch."

Lewis did not survive to return for that tobacco spitting visit. When I was departing I noticed several sets of rails Lewis would have had to clear with his disgusting spit. The more distant rails were not there when Lewis was alive. Sara commented that the wheelchair ramp to which those belong was for her late husband. Lewis would not have to clear those rails.

Maybe when I come back Sara will let me try my tobacco spitting skills over various sets of rails. If not, I will sure enjoy a visit on her porch. I will make sure Big Rich joins us so I behave myself with Gypsy Woman.

I grew up Presbyterian and have more recently been a Methodist. Moreland Baptists do not want or need another interdenominational scandal.

Carol Chancey, Jimmy Haynes & Winston Skinner

The day before I met with Sara Jane Skinner and H. Richard Smith at Sara's house I met with Carol Chancey at the Lewis Grizzard Museum in Moreland. Carol and I had spoken on the phone often and aspired to meet for weeks. Before she arrived I was thrilled to see Jimmy Haynes pull up, as he is the first person I met face to face on this Lewis Grizzard odyssey way back in November. You can thank or blame Jimmy for all this.

I cram that meeting into this chapter with Winston because Carol and Jimmy crammed themselves into my meeting with Winston. It was a cramming I hoped would happen but did not know to expect. No one tells me nothing. I just get ambushed and wish I took shorthand and/or brought more legal pads.

So never mind who said what when on whichever date we met. I just gotta get information on paper before my notes disintegrate.

Carol Chancey is a UGA journalism grad and manager of the Moreland Cultural Arts Alliance. That might sound fancy for a town of 400 people give or take, but that small town has a whole lot of arts to get in alliance.

Not only did Lewis Grizzard grow up in Moreland, so did Erskine Caldwell. Caldwell wrote The Bastard, Poor Fool, Tobacco Road

and God's Little Acre. Those
titles might make you think the
books could have been funny, like
if Lewis wrote them. I read all
four, and they are not funny. But
enough about unfunny Erskine.

Plus Moreland has a bunch of
general interest history. Carol
Chancey is the glue who ties
Lewis, Erskine and Moreland
general history together in one
building. She is very pleasant and
funny and she's a fellow Dawg, so
I should maybe not call her glue.
But she ain't here.

Jimmy Haynes is the stonewalling
sandbagging volunteer at the
Moreland Cultural Arts Alliance
public facility, also known as the
Lewis Grizzard Museum. The
building is a former lingerie mill
now undergoing magnificent
restoration due to the fine work
of Carol, Winston and probably
Jimmy. But Jimmy don't talk much.

Jimmy first told me he is a simple volunteer, Air Force veteran and not much else. Carol ratted him out. Jimmy has been treasurer or finance director for untold organizations. That means he knows where the bodies are buried. They probably choose him for such assignments because he is smart, a bit cagey and don't talk much.

The Moreland Cultural Arts Alliance is able to do such great things with the former lingerie mill because Carol, Winton and probably Jimmy if he would talk shrewdly set up a SPLOST program to fund much of the ambitious project. SPLOST is a special-purpose local-option sales tax for stuff like this. Maybe you know that and did not need it explained. I had to Google it. I have to Google a lot of things.

First, the Lewis Grizzard Museum
is actually in a former nylon
stockings mill. I call it a
lingerie mill because I think
Lewis would have preferred panties
over pantyhose, as do most men.
But let's not get into that.

The Moreland Cultural Arts
Alliance has a whole bunch more
Erskine and Lewis and Moreland
history stuff stored in locations
they will not reveal to me. Had I
bolted with that 100th anniversary
magazine Lewis helped write like I
wanted to would justify why they
won't tell me where stuff is. The
point is a lot more stuff will be
on display for the public to see
soon.

I wish I could say the University
of Georgia was leading such a
charge with Lewis stuff like this
town of 400 give or take. I get no
indication the Lewis stuff in
storage at UGA is coming out of

that storage during my lifetime.
Unless I break in and bolt with
it.

If one is to believe him, Jimmy
Haynes is now treasurer for only
the Moreland July 4 BBQ weekend
project. That includes generations
old proprietary top secret BBQ
recipes. Good thing Jimmy is in
charge and one of perhaps several
keepers of the recipes. I will be
there, and I started fasting now.
It is January.

Back to Moreland religious
conflict, Jimmy grew up Methodist
but as a youth crossed the line to
play in a Baptist baseball youth
league. As he wrote it elsewhere
but did not tell me, they needed
him as a triple threat. He could
not hit, run or field a grounder.
But he did manage to break up a
no-hitter as final batter in a
casual practice scrimmage. He
stuck his bat out, made contact

and the ball dropped for a bloop single. The pitcher was Lewis Grizzard, who I expect seethed about Jimmy for decades. Maybe that is why Jimmy claimed to not know Lewis well when I first met him.

By the way, I mentioned to Carol in Jimmy's presence that maybe I could ply him with adult beverages to loosen his tongue and get him yapping. He replied, "It will only take one." I like Jimmy more and more.

Back to the meeting with Winston. Oh yeah, Winston is also a Moreland Cultural Arts Alliance board member. We all tried to figure out how my Lewis book can help the Lewis Grizzard Museum and vice versa. We are still working on that. Carol, Jimmy and Winston rattled off names of other people who knew Lewis that I need to contact. I have yet to contact any because I do not have their numbers. They will likely have to wait until the addendum to this book - or the next book.

Digressing further, yesterday I got a call from Jackie Kennedy. I wrote it down as Canady because it was cold while I was walking around with my son around his baseball practice fields. I am pretty sure Jackie Kennedy is or was with Viking Press or Doubleday, but she said she was calling on behalf of the Newnan Times-Herald. Maybe she was sandbagging like Jimmy, or maybe she got sick of New York and wants to wind down and a great Southern town at a great Southern paper.

Jackie told me she is writing a magazine article to commemorate the 25th anniversary of Lewis Grizzard's death. Former editor Jim Minter of the Atlanta Journal and Constitution referred Jackie to me. When I told her I had met her own editor Winston that caught her by surprise. Glad I am not the only person being ambushed.

Jackie and I talked for about an hour. I think she said I am one of five or six people contributing to her piece. Unlike me Jackie is smart and learned to type while she talks. She says she needs 8,000 words. I gave her over 2,000. We agreed the publishers and editor just need to print a fatter magazine.

I did not say it on the phone, but in a followup email I suggested to Jackie that the Newnan Times-Herald sell their Lewis article to some publisher with a national scope. Like maybe Viking Press or Doubleday if Jackie did not burn her bridges before moving south.

All this is still getting hashed out, and I ain't the one doing the hashing. I could use a plate of corn beef hash on this frigid and blustery January night, but that will leave less room for Jimmy's July 4 BBQ.

Winston Skinner

Another guy I hoped to unite with
H. Richard Smith and Sara Jane
Skinner was Winston Skinner. It
was not so much getting him to
unite with them as it was to get
him with both of them and me. Sara
is Winston's mother, so they
likely unite pretty often. Perhaps
even occasionally with Richard.

Since Winston is still quite
busily employed editing the

Newnan-Times Herald he could not
break free to make a quartet out
of our trio. So I made an
appointment to see Winston at his
office the day after meeting Sara
and Richard. While waiting for
Winston I had a splendid
conversation with Newnan-Times
Herald's Sara Moore. She was
behind the front reception desk,
but she was so funny and charming
I expect she does way more than
only recep. Like maybe make sure
Winston is on time for
appointments, as she so capably
did that morning.

Since Winston's time was short I
had to gush real fast about
meeting with his mom and Big Rich
the day before. I could not ask
what it was like to grow up in
that cool house with such a cool
mom and a probably cool dad and
did he have brothers and sisters
or was he a spoiled only child and
a bunch of other questions.

Winston may have first met Lewis when he was a kid attending the Scott's Book Store signings with his mom. He met Lewis perhaps a dozen times in his life.

In Winston's early days as a journalist he had occasion to interview Lewis. Lewis did not typically enjoy interviews about his books, but with Winston it was different. Lewis seemed relaxed and appeared to enjoy himself. Maybe that was because he knew Winston to be an earnest young practitioner of the trade. Maybe it was because Winston was a local home town boy. My guess is it was because Lewis still had the hots for Winston's mom, Gypsy Woman. Do not alienate the son if you are sweet on the mother. Sage words to live by.

While chatting with Sara Moore before Winston arrived she

informed me of something I did not know. Lewis wrote one summer for the Newnan-Times Herald. She showed me a couple of Lewis photos from the paper's 150 year anniversary special edition magazine.

Only upon exiting did Winston and Sara inform me that what Lewis did that summer was write much of the paper's 100 year anniversary special edition magazine. They gave me a copy of the mass produced 150th anniversary magazine. They brought out a rare tattered copy of the 100th anniversary edition. When I asked why that was not reproduced in quantity Winston said they were talking about it. I accused him of being all talk, probably not the best way to score points with an esteemed newspaper editor.

I had no time to read the edition Lewis helped write. I did

volunteer to go to a local copy shop, dissect the magazine, make PDF images of each page then reassemble it to original tattered condition. But they would have to give me a bunch of quarters, plus I had no time to do it that day.

What I also did, and Sara Moore can attest to it, is pretend to bolt out the front door carefully clutching that collector's item original. Sara thought it was kinda funny. I was kinda considering to keep running, but I figured that would not be conducive to Newnan sales of my Lewis Grizzard book if I ever finish it.

Reluctantly, I handed the relic back to Sara, who I assume returned it to some vault where no one can lay eyes on it. That is the way with Lewis Grizzard relics. Everything is stored in dark archives under lock and key.

No one can see nothing. What is the stinking deal?

Sprayberry's BBQ

No trip to the vicinity of Lewis's youth would be complete without a visit to Newnan's Sprayberry's BBQ, "Family Owned and Operated Since 1926".

Of course I ordered the:

Lewis Grizzard Special
Barbecue sandwich, Brunswick stew, and onion rings.

Manager Jamey Keith met Lewis when he was a kid but did not remember those meetings well. I regret that

I did not note the charming
server's name. She knew nothing
about Lewis beyond his framed
newspaper columns adorning the
Sprayberry's walls. This does not
bode well for the future of our
country.

When I told Jamey I would meet
Richard Smith and Sara Jane
Skinner the next day he asked me
to tell them "hey".

Jamey reeled off a long list of
people I should call, including
elder Sprayberry's staff either at

their other restaurant or not working the night of my visit.

Per Jamey, I gotta see Donald Sprayberry, cartoonist and illustrator David Boyd, Dr. Bobby Lee at Lee-King Pharmacy, Newnan Historian Elizabeth Beers and Colleen somebody, also known as Miss Pearl. Go to Miss Pearl's YouTube channel for unadulterated instruction on proper southern decorum across a broad range of topics.

I have yet to meet anyone Jamey recommended.

Jamey pointed out that Lewis never ordered mac and cheese. But he let me get away with it and promised not to tell anyone. He said Lewis would have deemed their new mustard based sauce to be a crime against humanity.

On this topic I must disagree with Lewis. Sprayberry's original sauce is as vinegary as I have tasted anywhere and takes some getting used to. It must be applied lightly or your respiratory passages slam shut. I like the addition of the delicious mustard based sauce.

But here me now, loud and clear:

Rudy Connor of Smokey Q at Lake Lanier's Bald Ridge Marina cranks out killer BBQ that rivals Sprayberry's toe to toe. One is not better than the other. They are both superb and unique. The two are 80 miles and 2 hours apart, so one is no threat to the other.

In case you forget Rudy's name or Smokey Q simply Google "lewis grizzard lake lanier". Once I write for a PR client I never give up promoting that client.

Danny Neil

Danny Neil is my older brother's
and my UGA fraternity brother who
holds the distinction of being the
last of my brother's
contemporaries to get married. He
was and is a good looking guy, and
he was once very much a man about
town in Atlanta. As he would have
been about the same age as Lewis I
figured he may have an encounter
or two to share. Danny did not
disappoint.

As has become typical, when I called Danny at one of his several resort area residences he said he met Lewis once or twice, but the encounters were not noteworthy.

I asked him to let me be the judge of that and allow me to ask some questions. Danny consented.

"Tell me about the first encounter."

I know, readers like to see dialogue. But if I write this like chit chat I will never finish this book.

One New Year's Eve Danny and a date from Jacksonville Florida were at an Atlanta bar. He offered a general location but neither of us could name it. The place may have been Clarence Fosters or Carlos McGee's. I frequented both but have been away from Atlanta so

long I can no longer even find
Lenox Square without GPS.

Lewis walked in with a date who
was rather mundane by what Danny
thought to be Lewis's standards.
They sat at the bar next to Danny
and date with polite nods but no
introductions. Danny certainly
knew who Lewis was but did not let
on. He simply braced for possible
adventure. Adventure came, but not
in the way Danny expected, as in
telling of jokes and stories.

Adventure came in the form of
Lewis wasting little time to begin
blatantly hitting on Danny's date,
right in front of Danny and
Lewis's mundane date. When Lewis
either got nowhere and departed or
went to the restroom Danny told
his date who Lewis was. His date,
being from Jacksonville, was both
unaware and unimpressed. Thus ends
Danny Lewis story number one.

Story number two does not involve Lewis first hand. Danny was solo at another Buckhead area bar, this one tended by the legendary Pete the Northside Barkeep. It was not Harrison's, Pete's main haunt. Pete barkept at many Atlanta bars over the course of his career.

As Danny was enjoying an adult beverage an attractive woman took a seat beside him at the bar. In conversation he brought up his recent military career, which he had transitioned into civilian life as a fuel negotiator for airlines. Danny is not only an attractive guy, he is an enterprising professional, and the attractive woman was duly impressed. Before long she was not so subtly coming on to Danny. Danny began to imagine possibilities. Then the lady excused herself to go to the powder room.

Pete the Northside Barkeep stepped in to inform Danny that the woman was Lewis Grizzard's current girlfriend. By this time Danny was a more avid fan of Lewis's work. He did not want to complicate his own life, and he figures Lewis's life was already complicated enough without Danny stepping into a tryst with Lewis's main squeeze. His enthusiasm for the lady suddenly dampened, when she returned from the powder room Danny politely wished her well and said he had to depart. Maybe he let her down easy by saying he forgot about a load of laundry or a dog needing to be fed. Whatever, thus ends Danny/Lewis story number two, though Lewis was not really a part of it.

If you have followed me so far you may have already reached the conclusion that Danny Neil enjoys yet another unique distinction. He may be the only man on the planet who has had (A) Lewis hit on his date and(B) Lewis's girlfriend hit on him in entirely different years. There is no assurance of this. If anyone has a similar experience you know where to find me.

Danny is now a happily married man and can no longer be bothered with such nonsense. I thank him for allowing me to bother him, since I was a 9 year old brat when we first met. He could and should have told me to go away.

Gerard Gunhouse

Gerard Gunhouse was my friend from freshman year day one at UGA when campus housing by error assigned me to a Myers Hall dorm room with Kevin Margeson, Gerard's future roommate. Gerard and Kevin grew up only two miles away from me in Atlanta, but they were in Dekalb County and I was in Fulton. They were private school preppy guys, and I was a public school sewer rat. The freshman lodging confusion notwithstanding, had I remained Kevin's roommate and/or even down the hall from Gerard none of us would have become sophomores.

When the lodging issue got settled they moved me from 309 South to 309 Central. That allowed for distance and a barrier between our sections, plus I got Pete Matey as a roommate. Without Pete's good influence and help with a wretched

two semesters of Botany I would
not have become a sophomore. Where
was I? Oh yea, Lewis.

Back to Lewis in a minute. In our
post UGA early career days circa
1980 to 1984 Kevin, Gerard and I
palled around. A lot. We went on
annual fishing trips to the
Redneck Riviera with Jackie Rice,
Phil Armistead, Kevin's cousin
David Sheats and other hooligans.
I don't know if Lewis deep sea
fished, but he would have enjoyed
this crowd. Only I rarely saw
anyone but Kevin and Gerard except
on those trips even though
everyone lived in Atlanta.

When Kevin, Gerard and I went out
we often ended up at Churchill
Arms, Buckhead's only British Pub
at the time, due to Gerard being a
2nd generation Brit who could
interpret the warm beer menu. We
played darts badly and regaled in

European history where we likely got most facts wrong.

Kevin married young and well to Sara. I like them both a lot because they have a beach house close to Jacksonville and can host me for Georgia Florida games.

Gerard married slightly older and well to Sarah. I like them a lot because they have a big house in Vinings and can host me for … when I need to be near Vinings.

After Kevin married Gerard and I often pretended to be pre-med students and crashed graveyard shifts in the Grady Hospital operating room, but only after a few adult beverages. We were responsible for the death of no one, but one evening I had to discourage Gerard from doing wheelies in a wheelchair on a non OR floor.

It was a slow trauma night, and we went walking other floors to entertain ourselves. In our color coded scrubs people mistook us for young doctors and got out of our way as we strutted our tipsy selves down hallways. That was entertainment enough for me, but apparently not Gerard. He had to do wheelies, which I thought to be very undoctorlike.

Gerard parlayed that Grady experience and into a successful medical device sales career. The best thing is he met Sarah while doing that. She still works happily, and he is happily retired tinkering with a small fleet of classic Mercedes-Benz vehicles that he has never shown me, garaged off site somewhere. I want Gerard's gig, and I want Sarah. Too late for both.

Okay, back to Lewis. I correctly assumed Gerard may have crossed

paths with Lewis in his Buckhead
bachelor days after I departed for
Chicago. I called Gerard to
inquire about such. He claimed he
met Lewis but had nothing
interesting to contribute. I asked
him to let me be the judge of
that. I have my script down pat.

I learned that Gerard is the first
among my friends to have been a
regular at Lewis's favorite
watering hole, Harrison's. Gerard
was a regular because he dated a
bartender and could drink for
free. This is the first essential
step to retiring young and owning
more than one Mercedes-Benz. As
Gerard proves, employer buyouts,
stock options and a hyper
successful wife help later in
life, but free alcohol early in
life is where to start.

For the record, Gerard did not
date Pete the Northside Barkeep.
Gerard dated a female who barkept

alongside Pete. Gerard got to know Pete well and see Lewis often.

Gerard began telling the story he did not think interesting with the observation that Lewis was obnoxious, never paid for drinks and always had a crowd of people around him while he drank and told stories.

I stopped Gerard and asked him to describe Lewis's obnoxiousness. Gerard said at the beginning of the night Lewis arrived surly, got more fun as he became more lubricated and got surly again as he got too lubricated. I asked Gerard if that describes a whole lot of people we know. I told him about the rigors of Lewis's workday, often dealing with Yankee bosses and the like. Like Lewis, many leave work in a bad mood and get more happy with alcohol. Almost all humans get less happy with too much alcohol. Gerard and

I were in the minority. He and I
were happy drinkers unless someone
started doing wheelies in a
hospital and thus disrupting my
faux doctor persona.

I further explained to Gerard that
by Lewis's very presence at
Harrison's more customers went
there. He may have had a monthly
tab. The Atlanta newspapers may
have paid his Harrison's bill to
keep the content coming. One can
not know these things by simple
observation. Lewis was a generous
man, and one phone conversation
with Gerard Gunhouse was not going
to change that reality in my mind.
Gerard saw the light and agreed.
Then he waxed philosophical as I
knew the Gerard I once knew
eventually would if I got him
talking long enough. Or maybe he
waxed algebraic.

Gerard summarized that Lewis's
mood swings and alcohol

consumption interacted 'on a bell curve'. That stunned me, as I know Gerard was no math major, but maybe that private schooling left him with some sense of reason.

Again, I reminded Gerard that many drinking people perform much like Gerard described. No alcohol = surly. The right amount of alcohol = happy. Too much alcohol = surly again. Only happy drinkers like Gerard and I used to be are exceptions to this algebraic pattern.

Gerard again saw the light. Now that I drink ever so rarely it is a pleasure to have newfound clarity of thought and the ability to reality things down like I did on the phone that night with Gerard.

I will end this abruptly as my call with Gerard ended abruptly. The line went dead for no explicable reason. I called Gerard back and left a message for him to call me. His pattern is that he rarely returns a call less than 48 hours after one leaves a message, even if you just talked to him. Not only do he and Sarah travel internationally way too often, I expect he finds an urgent need to go tinker with his garage full of expensive vehicles.

Whichever, Gerard's good company, a wife way out of his class and excellent home in Vinings mean that he and I will be friends for life. At least from my perspective.

Newspapermen

Newspapermen make exceptional company.

You have probably not heard of me, but I am writing a biography of the late, great newspaperman, Lewis Grizzard. In recent weeks this project has led me to three other legendary newspapermen.

I hope and believe I will meet one or more legendary newspaperwomen along the way, though that has not happened yet. This article is about newspapermen.

The three newspapermen I speak of are, in alphabetical order, Jim Minter, Dink NeSmith and Carey Williams. Besides their decades of experience in the newspaper business, they have two things in common that are near and dear to my heart:

1. The University of Georgia
2. Lewis Grizzard

One of the three encouraged me to
revive the fading legacy of Lewis
Grizzard when all I was doing was
asking where Lewis's stuff was.
The other two offered invaluable
content, as by the time I met them
I had decided to write a book.

Meeting each of the three was a
most memorable event in its own
right. My time with them ranged
from 45 minutes to three hours. I
could have spent a week with any
of the three without running out
of things to talk about.

One is the retired editor of the
Atlanta Journal-Constitution.
Another owns one half of many
community newspapers in Florida,
Georgia and North Carolina. The
third owns, publishes, edits and
writes for a vibrant community

newspaper founded by his late
father.

Each of the three had incredibly
colorful stories to share about
Lewis Grizzard. Each referred me
to at least four other notable
people I need to talk to. They
made introductions to folks who
otherwise would not likely take my
call.

I firmly believe Messrs Minter,
NeSmith and Williams each need to
have a biography written about
them. In every five minutes of
conversation I could envision at
least one chapter. These men
seemingly know everyone and
everything of importance in the
state of Georgia - and beyond -
and they generously share what
they know with grace, humor, charm
and humility.

Let's go back and start with a
remarkable coincidence before I

began to write anything. I am a
Lake Lanier guy, and I assumed
Lewis spent some time at Lanier. I
Googled "lewis grizzard lake
lanier" and was astonished to find
that the top result was something
I wrote in 2017. It was an article
to promote Smoky Q, a BBQ joint at
Bald Ridge Marina that Lewis would
have loved.

I then called a friend at Lanier
who knew Lewis, only to discover
Lewis was a Lake Oconee guy. I
Googled "lewis grizzard lake
oconee", and the top result was a
video of Carey Williams telling a
rather colorful story about
experiences with Lewis. I set that
information aside.

(Please pardon the repeated image.)

In a completely separate incident, another guy loosely associated with Lewis sent me this photo. I met the very colorful guy who wrote that check. He was Lewis's Lake Oconee next door neighbor, golfing and gambling buddy. Lewis is the reason he bought a home at Oconee.

Carey Williams is the reason Lewis did a number of things. Along with the late, great Mickey Mantle, Carey is the reason Lewis bought a home at Oconee not long after they filled the lake. Let's say Mickey and Carey are each 50% responsible for Lewis's purchase decision.

More on Mickey Mantle and Lewis in some future column.

Carey Williams is 100% responsible for Lewis's decision to hire the late, great James Shannon as his driver for the last 10+ years of his life. Many have said I need to interview James. Only Carey informed me that James died one to two years after Lewis.

James Shannon drove Lewis in a stretch limousine for years. For years Lewis and friends would ride in back playing cards for money while enjoying their share of adult beverages. The check in the photo above may have been written in the back of that limousine.

Carey Williams and James Shannon are responsible for Lewis Grizzard being officially or unofficially deputized in a nearby county. Let's say Carey is 75% responsible, and James is 25% responsible. That deputization is reputed to have allowed James to drive citation-free for the remainder of Lewis's life.

Technically a legislator and sheriff of that nearby county deserve some credit for Lewis's deputization. I believe both to be deceased, but they likely still have family living nearby. Carey Williams is a civilian and a legendary newspaperman. He pretty much said I could write anything that was not profane about him, and he might very well publish it during a slow news week.

Google tells me that 800 words is about the maximum for a typical newspaper column. That means I better stop now at 800 without even telling any more great stories.

More to follow. Sorry, this last line makes 808 words.

Troy Beckett

I have had people tell me they had a Lewis experience they did not think was interesting. I asked them to let me be the judge of that and to explain what happened. More than three chapters have resulted from those discussions.

One was my 1985 UGA Phi Gam fraternity brother Troy Beckett. Though he graduated only six years after I did, Troy and I are not sure if we have met. He is an Athens native and lives there now, which makes me quite envious. Based on our first conversation it is good that Troy is a good financial advisor and I am the writer. Or at least I want to be a writer if someone will publish this.

"Good writer" would be better. I do not mean in terms of critical acclaim, which would be just fine. I mean in terms of people buying it. If people buy it critics can go wash socks as far as I am concerned.

Back to Troy and Lewis.

At age 17 Troy went to buy a book for his mom Wanda in Atlanta. He was surprised to see Lewis signing books and got in line. As he moved closer he figured out he was supposed to buy Lewis's book, but he was out of money. He stayed in line and expected Lewis to chew him out. When he plopped the book down Lewis looked up with a grin and said, "Good choice! She writes way better than I do."

I told Troy, "Damn. You have a collector's item! Thousands have Grizzard books signed by Grizzard. You very likely have the only Agatha Christie he ever signed." He got the point and claims his kids are now fighting over it.

Now, I warned Troy that his signed Agatha is not quite like Antiques Roadshow where someone discovers a Picasso under the ugly watercolor their weird cousin gave them in 1973. Or a Honus Wagner card they were about to attach to their kid's bicycle spokes to make the vehicle sound motorized. I could tell I was starting to lose Troy by talking like an old man even older than I am and got back to the point. His book ain't worth enough to retire on or even make a mortgage payment. But it is rare. Fortunately, the financial advisor in him preempts acting on anything I said.

So with all of this in mind I am
writing many chapters on people I
know with the assumption that will
lead to at least one book sale.
Hopefully those people have
relatives who do not hate them and
may also buy the book. The minimum
qualification to score a chapter
is an interesting encounter with
Lewis.

And I am finding almost any
encounter with Lewis can be made
interesting enough to score a
chapter. Particularly if the
individual and I collude to
embellish details like Lewis did
and about which only the
individual and I know are
embellished. But with a photo like
Wanda's above, who can prove we're
lying?

Bobby Griffin

There was a time when I thought Lake Lanier's Bobby "ScubaMan" Griffin's greatest claim to fame was showing up on short notice and failing to recover a houseboat deck chair my son bonehead Ben left in a place where a gust of wind could blow it overboard and to the 65 foot depths beneath our dock at Bald Ridge Marina. My target was large and I figured a cinch to find in a small search area. I learned it ain't that simple. It is pitch black 30 feet down and even pitch blacker 65 feet down. He charged me $35 for failing to find a chair that likely had a depreciated value of $7.23. But my matching set of four became a set of three, meaning bonehead Ben had to stand or sit on the flybridge if we had company over for movie night.

The following year Bobby achieved somewhat greater fame for failing to recover Julio Jones's diamond stud earring. The thing is, with that earring Bobby's target was microscopic, and the search area was like, all of Lake Lanier. You see, the loser of the jewelry was wave running and at some point noticed his earlobe felt about a pound lighter. That allows for a debris field totaling several acres. In the case of Lake Lanier, 38,000 acres give or take depending on recent rainfall and/or shore erosion caused by wave running athletes in no wake zones. But the value of that target ranged from $35,000 to six figures plus based on which report you read. I gather Bobby charged more than $35 because TV cameras were there, meaning he may have had to join the Screen Actors Guild.

The moral to that story is I now tell my sons and their friends to always remove all $35,000 to six figures plus diamond stud earrings before they go wave running.

It turns out Bobby had a far greater claim to fame than either of these impressive if unsuccessful exploits. He once spent a day and night hanging around with Lewis Grizzard. And that was long before Bobby was ScubaMan or anything remotely resembling ScubaMan.

Bobby was invited to this swanky wedding not because some goofball lost something not findable at the bottom of some murky body of water. No, Bobby was invited because he married a hot babe who was a bridesmaid to the hot bride in that swanky wedding.

The wedding was so swanky it was held on an Atlantic Ocean island. That may have spelled search and rescue opportunities for Bobby, but everyone on that island was so affluent they used diamond studded earrings instead of clay pigeons for target practice. Well, not really, but almost.

Lewis was invited as a friend of a friend on such short notice he did not bring a date. That must mean something like .273 seconds advance notice if Lewis did not have time to find a date. They dispatched a helicopter to pick him up on the mainland.

The groom, who barely knew Lewis, asked him to say a few words at the rehearsal dinner. Lewis obliged and asked what topic the groom would like for Lewis to address. The groom suggested, "How about the sanctity of marriage?"

To which Lewis replied, "Are you sure? Isn't that about like inviting Idi Amin to your buffet?"

Yes, this is a story repeated elsewhere. And it bears a repeated explanation for readers who never studied history. Idi Amin was a Ugandan dictator rumored to be a cannibal. It really ruins a joke when you have to explain it.

One thing not repeated elsewhere is Lewis's comment to Bobby, shared sometime over the course of the weekend when only Lewis and Bobby were hanging together. Lewis observed that he never saw so many millionaires with ponytails in his life. He was not talking about the women, most of whom were millionaires only by marriage past, present or future to male millionaires with ponytails. Either way, Lewis by this time was pretty well heeled himself, as were many of his friends. Only most of Lewis's millionaire friends shunned ponytails.

Lewis wrote about the wedding in a column, including the ponytail line he first tested on Bobby. But guess what? I can't find that column, nor can Bobby, who swears he saved it and has it in storage somewhere.

Many of those in the wedding party have built larger fortunes and are extremely philanthropic, and virtually every male has shed his ponytail. One guy has an estimated net worth exceeding $250 million. He personally built a Lake Lanier houseboat large enough for the groom from that wedding to land his personal helicopter on the flybridge until the US Corps of Engineers put a stop to that. The Corps owns all of Lake Lanier and tries to put a stop to even much smaller fun flying things, such as drones. But don't get me started on that topic.

I once owned what my friends and I thought was a pretty big houseboat. But its flybridge was hardly large enough to hold a chair. Forget about trying to land a chopper on that thing. Plus, my boat sank with only the help of a leaky water heater valve. Even a paper airplane might have sent the vessel to the floor of Lake Lanier on a bad day. And yes, that was a bad day.

Time to wrap up this tale of Bobby ScubaMan Griffin's epic Lewis weekend and move on to the next chapter.

The Internet

I often wonder what Lewis could have achieved with the internet. It was certainly around when he was alive, yet no one I have spoken to said he ever used it.

The internet is essential to my research on Lewis. Part of what alarms me is how much Lewis stuff is NOT on the internet. But there is plenty there, and I have found some gems. It only takes creative use of search terms.

I was particularly surprised to find this:

lewis grizzard essay
Валентин Евдокимов

Had I discovered this earlier it would have saved a lot of time and effort. Instead of interviewing a whole bunch of people in person and by phone apparently I could just contact Валентин Евдокимов, and he or she would do all this for me. And cheap.

But even this required some research. The link took me to a provocative headline:

Write My Essay - Cheap Writing Service 24/7

And the details revealed this:

Professional "Write my Essay" Service

Deadline for the essay making you nervous? Our online platform provides the essay service on time and budget. We are focused on delivering high-quality academic texts to students from the US and all over the world. Thanks to our academic writing superstars, we have helped thousands of people submit original high-quality works, and we can help you too!

STUDENT PLACES AN ORDER

WRITERS MAKE THEIR OFFERS

STUDENT HIRES A WRITER

THE WRITER GETS TO WORK

Wow. The possibilities seem endless. But my guess is offshore writers like Валентин Евдокимов

are who make those offers.
Валентин Евдокимов does not sound
like anyone from Moreland GA or
even Newnan. If they are from
Moreland, do they go to Lewis's
Methodist church or the Baptist
church? Or might they be one of
the Presbyterians who Morelanders
ran out of town?

Lewis once wrote about an offshore
person he recruited in his hotel
lobby. He was in Costa Rica, and
an attractive 'working woman'
offered to do anything he wanted
for $100. "Anything?", Lewis
asked. "Yes, anything." He then
handed the lady a $100 bill and
the key to his room. "Go up and
write my Sunday column."

Records do not show whether she
wrote his column. But my guess is
the essay service above is cheaper
because writers compete for the
work. To my knowledge the Costa

Rican woman's offer was not part of a bidding process.

Having some experience with e-commerce, I can attest that Costa Rica is not the least expensive place to find a virtual assistant or whatever, and I assume it is not the least expensive place to find a writer. Wherever Валентин Евдокимов lives is probably cheaper.

Further, the services the Costa Rican woman initially had in mind are not yet available by e-commerce. But that may change soon. E-commerce companies continue to innovate, and soon one may be able to have a Costa Rican delivered to one's door by drone within hours of placing one's order. Particularly in Atlanta, a market where such innovations are often introduced first.

But Lewis tried to pay for writing, not what that woman had in mind, so let's get back to e-commerce writing.

I looked to see if the website guarantees a certain grade but concluded I am too far down this rabbit hole already. If they do offer a guarantee, this is what I would demand instead of an A or B term paper: 100% actual documented interviews with hard to find friends of Lewis Grizzard resulting in a well written and highly popular book that remains on the New York Times bestseller list for a minimum of three years. Or Oprah recommends it. The real Oprah, not some virtual offshore Oprah. Otherwise I am not that picky.

Speaking of cheating, even though we haven't used that word yet, Lewis cheated when he wrote columns. More accurately, he helped other people cheat. More accurately, he wrote other people's columns when they called in sick. They didn't necessarily ask him to, he just did it even if no one necessarily asked him.

Lewis also cheated for that editor. Though technically perhaps this should not be called cheating. If the editor had to travel to cover some big story he asked Lewis to edit the paper in his absence. He was always nervous to return and not for reasons one might expect. Imagine trusting Lewis Grizzard to do anything unsupervised if your job depended on it, particularly if the product is a major metropolitan newspaper read by millions. That was not the issue here. The issue here is that editor in question often realized the papers Lewis edited were edited better than the guy who got paid to edit would have edited them.

As best I have learned, Lewis only cheated in a column once, or so he said. That was another newspaperman's column on Pep Stone having not gone to his farm one day and learning it had been robbed clean the day he did not go there. Lewis liked the column, and he told owner and writer Carey Williams of the Greensboro Georgia Herald-Journal that was the only other person's column Lewis ever republished in its entirety. If someone can find another, let's see it.

Carey Williams also advises that Lewis would fool readers, though that can not be called cheating. Regardless of what he did or how late he stayed up the night before, Lewis would awaken and start writing at 5 AM. That might involve watching CNN to see if anything interesting happened, then writing about some event as if he was there. Lewis would put his slant on what CNN said, and no reader ever knew he was not on the scene.

Which brings us back to Lewis paying either the Costa Rican lady or other writers to cheat in general. If Lewis wanted a writer to write like he sometimes did, that is to watch CNN and write based on that, Lewis would probably have to pay a lot more. Lewis would deem watching the CNN of today to be torture. Lewis could be a jerk on occasion, but no one I have talked to says he was a sadist. Were the writer for hire to be forced to watch MSNBC even Lewis would not be able to afford it, nor would he likely ever ask anyone to watch MSNBC.

So what is the point you ask? Lewis went down enough rabbit holes with zero use of the internet. Imagine if Lewis had access to college football websites where you scroll down to see headlines like this:

7 Engagement Rings that are Works of Art | Brilliant Earth

Such sites inevitably lead to a slideshow that takes hours to navigate even if you have better than the dial up speed of Lewis's day. Imagine if the photo enticing people to go to such a site was of a nearly nekkid woman, as such sites so often employ. And after you take hours to navigate the site there ain't no nearly nekkid women anywhere to be found. You want to shoot yourself for having looked at a bunch of overpriced bling when you've already told the world that instead of ever marrying again you are just going to find a woman you don't like and give her a house.

Thus concludes our essay, written by us, honest, on Lewis Grizzard and the internet.

Sugar Bowls

Lewis Grizzard and I attended four Sugar Bowls together. More accurately, we attended the same four Sugar Bowls. Unfortunately for me we attended them separately and in very different styles.

The first was my freshman year, the only season I attended as a UGA undergraduate. I recall only that I stayed in a dive hotel, my otherwise hot date wanted me to find other accommodations and Pittsburgh's Tony Dorsett ran all over the Junkyard Dawgs. Lewis was somewhere in the audience of 76,117, and we did not connect.

Suffice it to say Lewis and I never connected at any Sugar Bowl. Lewis's 1977 date very likely did not have to ask for better accommodations, but that is not to say Lewis did not get into hot water with romance companions for other reasons, as I will reveal.

If my chronology is correct in 1977 Lewis would have been with wife number two from Chicago, implying she would have no grasp of or appreciation for SEC football, but I have no record of Lewis's Sugar Bowl experience that year. It may or may not account for the brevity of marriage number two.

I have several accounts from Shelton Stevens, Bobby Poss and others of Lewis and cohorts traveling to and from New Orleans by RV, a mode of transportation I could never get any of my Sugar Bowl quorums to agree to. Either we could not scrounge up the deposit to reserve far enough in advance or we intended that RV to also be our sleeping accommodations - and our dates would not agree to the latter. Or

a combination thereof. Lewis and
his cohorts never had to stoop so
low as to propose to their females
that they lodge in an RV. Again,
far different budgets and travel
styles between Lewis and me.

My next Sugar Bowl with (and
without) Lewis is the one where I
can not believe I did not run into
him, as he made his presence well
known via very conspicuous stunt.
This was the glorious 1980
National Championship season, my
first as a season ticket holder a
year after graduation. Tickets and
decent but cheapest available
French Quarter lodging via the
official UGA office.

On the New Year's Eve in question
Lewis approached a sidewalk Lucky
Dog vendor and asked if he could
sell the Lucky Dogs while the
vendor watched. The vendor
expressed distrust, licensing
complications and other reasons

why that could not happen. Lewis
solved the dilemma by buying the
vendor's entire inventory, perhaps
the cart itself, for perhaps what
the vendor paid for an entire
year.

Lewis proceeded to hawk Lucky Dogs
all night long, and that is where
I should have seen him. With
lodging within walking distance,
my date and I traversed the entire
French Quarter for many hours, and
I think we dined on nothing but
Lucky Dogs. Shelton Stevens
relates that Lewis encountered one
problematic patron who repeatedly
requested relish for her Lucky
Dog. After repeatedly insisting he
had no relish she complained that
a vendor down the street offered
relish. To which Lewis replied,
"Then take your ass down the
street and buy your Lucky Dog from
that guy." One can hardly blame
him, and I can say with reasonable

certainty that lady was not my
date.

If my chronology is correct
Lewis's companion that year would
have been wife number three. Again
per Shelton, Lewis's date tired of
Lewis's antics and retired early
to their hotel room. Maybe she was
not a fan of Lucky Dogs or tired
of Lucky Dog jokes. In the wee
hours when Lewis's Lucky Dog
inventory was depleted Lewis was
reluctant to go to his hotel room
and face his companion's music.
Shelton and others assured him she
would be asleep and all would be
okay. Lewis boarded the elevator,
but those with him wanted to make
certain he went to his room and
waited on the lobby level. Sure
enough, when the elevator returned
Lewis was still on it. He had the
elevator phone in his hand and
asked that one of the party talk
to his companion. Never in the
history of elevator phones had one

connected to a guest room, and this was no exception. The party escorted Lewis to his room, helped him unlock the door and shoved him inside.

The next day was National Championship glory and triumph over Notre Dame. All I can say about that is Lewis partied until at least 2 AM in Vince and Barbara Dooley's suite. My date and I were not invited.

Sugar Bowl year three was for me memorable for only two reasons. We again lost to Pittsburgh, and I was certain my otherwise very hot date was going to land us in jail. I did not know her well, and bad vibes started early when I was pulled over for speeding in my Datsun 280Z at a notorious I-10 speed trap in Pascagoula Mississippi. Before I was even safely stopped on the shoulder she said, "Let me talk to that pig. I hate pigs." I may have stuck socks in her mouth and sealed it with duct tape. I do not recall getting lucky that trip, and I never saw that woman again. We lost again to Pittsburgh, and I again did not connect with Lewis.

Sugar Bowl year four gets confusing. We lost to Penn State, I was with a hot date that respected law enforcement even as much as I did, and I would swear we lodged with a friend who lived in the NOLA Garden District. He warned us to either drive ourselves to the Quarter on New Year's Eve or not go due to a looming transit strike at midnight. We scoffed at his advice and took the trolley into town. Sure enough there was a strike, and no cab could be hailed no matter how much cash you waved. We called my pissed off friend out of bed, and he picked us up driving in nothing more than jockey shorts to stress his level of irritation. I doubt Lewis encountered any such inconvenience that night or ever, and I did not see him to ask.

The confusion here is that I find no reference to a 1980s Sugar Bowl transit strike. I do see reference to a 1975 strike, but that year I was in town at the dive lodging a very different date found objectionable. My guess is the 1980s incident was only short lived to annoy tourists and my Garden District host, not long enough to merit internet mention.

When my attention span warrants I will reveal tales of Lewis's disgruntled romantic companions and/or vehicular malfunctions to or from New Orleans and similar adventurous road trips.

I was on none of them, but I now know people who were.

Pepper Rodgers

Lewis Grizzard wrote all sorts of things about Georgia Tech over the years, one of which was that he did not have enough pimples to get in.

Thus, I was surprised when Jim Minter informed me that there was a stint when Lewis became a borderline Tech fan. It was due to his close friendship with football coach Pepper Rodgers.

Pepper almost made a Tech fan out of me as well, and I was a UGA undergrad when Pepper coached the Jackets. You could not help but like Pepper. He was always smiling and cracking incredibly funny lines.

Pepper played at Tech and came back to coach after impressive seasons at UCLA. He lamented upon his return that only then did he discover Tech had not improved a single football facility since his 1950s playing days.

Lewis and Pepper became friends on the tennis court. Pepper claimed to be pretty good at tennis for a football coach, and Lewis was pretty good for a newspaper columnist. They competed on Pepper's Buckhead home court and at the Bitsy Grant Tennis Center.

My natural question to Pepper was if he frequented Buckhead after hours venues with Lewis. He did not, other than ducking in every now and then. Pepper was competitive at a lot of things, but late night prowling and adult beverage consumption were never among them.

Pepper recalls being with Lewis on one impactful day in both of their lives. They were at the beach in Hilton Head on August 16, 1977 listening to some band. One of the musicians interrupted their performance to announce that Elvis had died. Pepper and Lewis were both avid fans, and that put both into a funk for the remainder of their vacation.

Georgia Tech fired Pepper in 1979, ending what little affinity Lewis had for the North Avenue trade school. Pepper went on to a colorful stint as a professional coach of the USFL Memphis Showboats, where he took them to the playoffs in their second and final year.

Pepper returned a decade later to coach the Mad Dogs, Memphis's one year wonder during the Canadian Football League's failed attempt to invade the US. Both the Showboats and Mad Dogs were part owned by the Elvis estate. The Liberty Bowl surface area was too small to accommodate the larger CFL playing field, and players would literally run into brick walls. Pepper kept the atmosphere light by pretending not to understand convoluted CFL rules at critical points during a game.

Sadly, Pepper's Mad Dogs season was 1995, the year after Lewis died. Though not a particular fan of pro football, one can only imagine what Lewis would have written about Canadians attempting

to introduce their alien version
of the game south of the Mason
Dixon line. There would be
inevitable comparison to Yankee
carpetbaggers, save the fact that
Canadians are infinitely more
likable than Yankees.

Among Pepper's many protégés was
Steve Spurrier, who he hired as a
young assistant to handle Tech
quarterbacks. Pepper may be
responsible for Spurrier staying
in the coaching profession, as at
the time Spurrier was not certain
it was what he wanted to do.
Bulldog fans might cite that as a
reason to resent Pepper, but it
apparently did nothing to perturb
Lewis.

Pepper says his Virginia living
room is pretty much wall to wall
framed photos with celeb friends
like Mark Harmon, Reggie White,
Spurrier and Lewis. His favorite
is a 1996 20th Anniversary edition

of Memphis Magazine with Pepper
sharing cover space with The King.

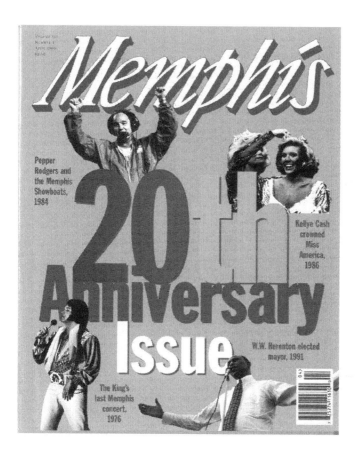

I doubt that Lewis would object to
second place behind Elvis.

Residences

Lewis Grizzard famously resided in two Athens domiciles that I can identify, Reed Hall and Callaway Gardens apartments. This leads me to document my four domiciles in case anyone wants to know decades down the road.

By stroke of luck I applied to Myers Hall as my freshman year dorm. It appealed because it was not a dreaded high rise and it was coed. The coed aspect paid zero dividends, as females were in a separate wing with impenetrable barriers keeping males at bay. Oh well.

Yet Myers held several benefits I did not foresee before even moving to Athens. One was that it was across the street from Phi Gamma Delta, the fraternity of my future. Another was roommate Peter

Bruce Matey, without whose help I may never have become a sophomore.

Upon arrival at Myers they by error put me in room 309 West with roommate Kevin Margeson. Kevin quickly became and remains a great friend, but had he remained my roommate I would have never become a sophomore. When we discovered UGA housing screwed up they moved me to room 309 Center. Gerard Gunhouse became Kevin Margeson's roommate. Had I roomed even near Gerard and Kevin I would have never become a sophomore. Kevin and Gerard went on to extraordinary career success, but they each departed UGA early to secure Georgia State degrees closer to the safety of their parents' homes.

With Pate Matey I stood a good chance at passing botany, a course some other idiot suggested would be both interesting and easy. It was neither. I was thinking horticulture like flowers and shrubs. Botany is monocots, dicots and cellular plant detail even more difficult and less interesting than monocots and dicots. Pete Matey was a seed agronomy major who got off on things like monocots and dicots. He never got me to get off on them, but without him I would never have made a B in Botany 101 and C in Botany 102.

On at least one occasion we were able to schlep an unfinished keg from the Phi Gamma Delta house across Lumpkin Street to Pete's and my Myers dorm room. This made us immensely popular for a night or two and even more remorseful that impenetrable barriers separated males from females in the Myers East wing. Pete Matey was also a moderate partier and good influence on a number of levels, further enhancing my chances of becoming a sophomore. Pete went on to extraordinary international career success in a variety of agriculture businesses. Whether he put monocot or dicot expertise to use in that career I have yet to find out. Since graduation I have seen Pete for a total of 7 minutes at a Who concert in Gwinnett county. The subject of monocots and dicots did not come up.

My sophomore year was the welcome and fraternally obligatory residence at Phi Gamma Delta. Phi Gams enjoyed a unique arrangement of having a separate apartment building adjacent the main lodge. Both buildings were then dumps, but residing in an apartment apart from the lodge was more conducive to a sophomore becoming a junior. My apartment was one of only two two bedroom apartments, which I deemed also preferable to a one bedroom. Having a single hooligan snoring three feet away was better than having three other hooligans snoring equally close. At least in my opinion. Please do not ask the hooligan next to whom I slept.

Our apartment was dubbed the Opium Den and had been dubbed that for at least a year before I resided there. To my knowledge no one who ever resided there imported a brown, sticky narcotic from Afghanistan. If they did I did not inhale it. I will make no further statement here about anything else I may or may not have inhaled. But it wasn't opium that I may or may not have inhaled.

Which brings me back to unfinished kegs. I do not recall there being any unfinished kegs during my sophomore year, which is unfortunate as it would be much easier to schlep a keg to the Opium Den than it was to Myers Hall room 309C. One would not have to cross Lumpkin Street without getting run over by a semi for one thing.

One reason we had no unfinished kegs my sophomore year was the Delta Deuteron Pledge Class, an unusually large and unwieldy group of young men who could consume an unusually large quantity of beer per capita. I was Pledge Trainer to the Delta Deuterons, but I claim no responsibility for instructing them on beer consumption. They pledged Phi Gam already more than capable in that department. They were also responsible for Phi Gam earning a number of athletic, academic and campus leadership awards despite being a very disobedient collection of young men. Their disobedience led to me never being appointed Pledge Trainer or elected anything else for the remainder of my Phi Gam days.

Delta Deuterons are now some of the most scary successful Phi Gams to ever emerge from any university anywhere. Amazingly, three stellar pastors emerged from their ranks. That is a good thing, because the rest need to repent. They can attribute their collective prosperity to me and remarkably successful assistant Pledge Trainer, Steve Anderson, who humbly asks to no longer be called Weasel. Hi Weasel!

Another thing about unfinished kegs. I bet there were none of those at Lewis Grizzard's Sigma Pi house. I can't really explain why there was one or two at the Phi Gam house. Maybe it was an Easter Sunday. Or maybe it was because Lewis was feverishly writing and editing in Atlanta and never dropped by our house.

My junior year residence was a scary house on Sunset Drive, far off Athens campus. I chose to live there because one Opium Den resident who resided at the Opium Den the year before I did needed a roommate because another former Opium Den resident graduated and left. Plus it was cheap, and I got a private bedroom for the first time and only one roommate in an entirely different bedroom. This would be almost like living back home again, but without my parents anywhere nearby to enforce rules like having to wake up before 2 PM.

The only drawback to residing on Sunset Drive was that my roommate concluded he had done his entire share of mowing the lawn and washing dishes the year before I moved in. I did both of those chores until I was no longer willing to do either again until the other guy got off his arse and did one or the other just once, if only out of good faith. The result was that he expressed good faith, well, never. We learned we could each stubbornly hunker down and do nothing just as well as the other. But we were otherwise best buds unless I went into his room and made awful noises on his saxophone without permission.

Grass grew waist high and dishes piled up in the sink. We eventually just roped of the kitchen as a toxic waste room and future Superfund site. You can imagine how this impressed dates we brought home, as in it did not. It seemed to bother only my dates, not my roommate's dates. Go figure.

Only when it came time to move out and collect a security deposit did roomie see fit to do his duty. He took down grass with a swing blade and needed more than a day to do it. He piled the toxic waste dishes into trash bags and hauled them to a landfill. I made sure to be far away when all such work took place. I had no stake in the security deposit, and the disgusting conditions were not my doing.

One bonus of residing on Sunset Drive was my roomie's friends were friends of John Mooney, at the time Athens's most celebrated murder suspect. I knew John Mooney, as did many UGA students. But I knew him as a customer at his pizza restaurant, not his friend. My roomie's friends called Mooney in jail with me listening on the other phone. I thought that was kinda cool, except in all likelihood Mooney was guilty of killing TK Harty, who I also knew, at the time Athens's most celebrated murder victim.

Mooney was indeed guilty, though not yet convicted when I had fun listening in on his jailhouse phone call. Maybe he would have been found not guilty had he talked to a lawyer instead of anyone at our house. I am pretty sure that was not Mooney's "one call", but still.

An almost spanking new River Mill Apartment was the site of my senior year residence. I chose it because my two roommates had furniture, whereas I had maybe a bed. Their furniture was a combination of rickety heirloom antiques and chrome and faux leopard skin disco, a motif combo that did not work well even in the 1970s.

But it was better than me having to buy anything, I could again walk to Sanford Stadium, and I got the cheapest smallest bedroom with no windows but a bathroom I could refuse to let the other two guys ever enter. That particular year a bedroom with no windows and a

hyper private bathroom were a boon
to my existence and sanity in ways
I will wait to divulge in some
future discussion.

Several parties at that River Mill
apartment were so embarrassing on
so many levels I dare not confess
participation even though no one
involved has insisted that I not
talk or write about them. Okay,
scratch that. There was a tequila
party that resulted in a bunch of
guys standing butt nekkid on our
balcony long after all females had
left the party. I was not one of
them. I had retired hours earlier
to barricade myself in my
windowless fortress bedroom,
emerging only when necessary to do
essential post tequila bathroom
activities in my hyper private
fortress bathroom.

The least embarrassing party we
hosted involved star UGA football
players who arrived at our crib

before any women arrived. Buck Belue was one of them, and all football players attended at the behest of a friend who was a scholarship tennis player. The football players were cordial and generously plied with a vast array of adult beverages we offered. Yet our assurances that hot females would arrive at any moment eventually lost credibility, and the football team bolted for destinations unknown.

Perhaps it was that they were remarkably disciplined and punctual, having been coached by Vince Dooley and Erk Russell. But you would think they would know there has never been any such thing as a disciplined and punctual UGA coed unless you are talking about ROTC cadets, none of whom did we invite that night, at least that I can recall. They were rare in 1979 in Athens, as there was no draft or other compelling

reason to join ROTC, whether male
or female.

But females we invited did indeed
arrive, not long after the
footballers departed. Many of
those females soon departed in
search of the recently departed
footballers, despite the fact we
could not tell them where the
footballers went. Maybe they
trusted their female sense of
smell, even though all of the
footballers were well groomed and
had obviously bathed since any
previous football practice or
weight room activity.

Remember now that this was the one
year away from a National
Championship football team, so
maybe that quality carries a
certain aroma. My date is
fortunately not one who departed,
for reasons I can not recall.
Maybe it was because she knew if I
got lucky and she got unlucky

later there would be no witnesses due to my windowless fortress bedroom.

This was not the night that a bunch of males ended up butt nekkid on our balcony with no females anywhere around. That was another night, again far more embarrassing than the night just described.

One last parting thought about my senior year at River Mill. I was President of the Marketing Club, later embellished on job applications as the University of Georgia Collegiate Chapter of the American Marketing Association. One of my roommates was a pre-med guy needing to polish up his GPA for med school, so he briefly became a business major. To further polish up chances of med school acceptance he asked if he could be my VP of the Marketing Club. When he subsequently failed to do his minimal job as VP, which was to fetch a keg, I fired him and offered to sign a statement to that effect on his med school applications. I was pissed because I had to fetch that keg, something I had done as VP the previous year and did not want to do as President. He is an MD today, but I fired his sorry ass in 1979. And it was a true pleasure to do so.

Thus concludes my thesis on University of Georgia residence locations. Though I was not writing newspaper columns and living Lewis Grizzard's legendary UGA life, I like to think my UGA life included some remarkable and colorful residences and experiences. Even diehard Lewis enthusiasts might agree, particularly if I choose to tell stories thus far omitted. But Lewis was known for being semi discrete, so I will aspire to be semi discrete. At least for the time being.

International Fame

We all know the internet was around when Lewis Grizzard was alive because in 1999 Al Gore blabbed on CNN to have taken the initiative to invent it years earlier. Thankfully, Al disappeared not too long thereafter.

From what everyone I have talked to tells me, Lewis never used the internet. Perhaps because he could not figure out how to get at it via either his Royal or Remington manual typewriter.

But I do use the internet, and today it led me to this:

Is your garden summer ready?
What to grow indoors, on balconies and windowsills now, to reap the rewards later

Writer Lewis Grizzard said: "It is difficult to think anything but pleasant thoughts while eating a home-grown tomato." You learn to appreciate amazing fresh flavours when you grow your own food — and with no plastic wrapping it is a guilt-free trip.

This is a March 2018 piece from a daily London England publication owned by a Russian. What Lewis would have to say about that circumstance is anyone's guess.

Maybe Al Gore is holed up at that Russian's house helping to hack American elections on some private server in the basement. Or maybe that Russian is responsible for the 2000 pregnant chads in Florida that spared the world from having Al Gore as President of the United States. Election hacking is so murky one may never know the truth.

I voted as a Floridian in that 2000 election even though I lived in Pennsylvania at the time. That was by virtue of owning property on the Redneck Riviera and wanting to vote in a state where I could make a difference. I made sure the chads on my legal and unhacked absentee ballot were as pure as the brownish November Philadelphia driven snow. In other words, they were not pregnant.

But back to the London newspaper. I wonder if home and gardening author Alex Mitchell knew Lewis and got that quote directly over a few pints and remembers it all these years later. My guess is not, as England is not generally known for fresh any kind of food, and Lewis was not apt to talk about tomatoes after a few pints.

My guess is Mr. Mitchell used the internet to look up pithy quotes about fresh tomatoes, and that's

where he found Lewis. The fact
that Lewis is there to be found is
rather ironic since I thus far
find no evidence that Lewis was
syndicated outside the United
States. Maybe Canada, probably not
Mexico. But Britain?

Lewis disliked Yankees, and Brits
dislike Yanks. I am pretty sure
their dislike and the people
disliked are two completely
separate subjects. Either way, it
seems unlikely Brits would
appreciate Lewis's humor, whether
they were Tommies, Poms, Limeys or
Kippers.

Another thing about Lewis and
foreign countries. I can't find
out which all he went to or why he
went to them. In 1985 he traveled
to the Soviet Union. Maybe that
was because the Beatles sang,
"Moscow girls really knock me out
… ", but Lewis was not a known
Beatles fan. Still, that would not

deter him from the pursuit of exotic love. Maybe he went there on an assignment for one of his employers.

To get to the bottom of this I demanded lunch with Jim Minter, former Atlanta Journal-Constitution editor. More accurately I begged. Well not really, he invited me and did so politely. But let's not split hairs. Let's say I went into that lunch with an inquisitive and demanding journalistic nose for the facts.

It didn't take long to get the facts. Jim Minter and the AJC had nothing to do with the Russia trip. Lewis went there on his own with stepbrother Ludlow Porch. That takes us back to possible pursuit of exotic love. But unlike Lewis, Ludlow was a happily married man, so nix that.

Jim speculated that they might have gone on a University of Georgia group trip. Since all of UGA's Lewis stuff is deep in storage I might find the truth there by maybe the 22nd century.

Or I could ask Ludlow Porch's widow. Yet Ludlow Porch was not his real name. He changed it to something mainstream because no one could spell or pronounce Bobby Hanson. I found Nancy anyway, only she never met Lewis. She is Ludlow's a/k/a Bobby's second wife, and she began dating Ludlow a/k/a Bobby the year after Lewis died. I am to speak with her in the next 64 hours, but in the meantime she wants me to read Ludlow's book, Lewis and Me and Skipper Makes Three.

Quick research on that book says, "so who better than Porch to reveal all the tales Grizzard never told on himself." In my opinion that should end with a questions mark, but I'll let it go. What concerns me more is that book might render my book useless. My book may be useless to begin with, but not so conspicuously so until now. I wish Lewis people would stop asking me to read books. Who has time to read books? Notice proper use of the question mark.

So do go out and buy <u>Lewis and Me and Skipper Makes Three</u>, but not until after you have bought, paid for and read my book. Otherwise, please disregard this paragraph and the two above. Pretend they do not exist.

This brings us back to Lewis and international fame, or lack thereof. Even if I don't read the book she wants me to Nancy better be prepared to answer some tough questions within 64 hours. She better not try to confuse me with

the excuse that she was not yet
around when Lewis and Ludlow were
up to their Soviet mischief.

At some point I must discuss
wisdom teeth, which have nothing
to do with international fame but
a lot to do with the Lewis, the
Soviet Union, London and a
vacation shrouded in mystery with
some guy named Ludlow.

Ken Murphy

Ken "Murph" Murphy is my hero for more reasons than I can list here. But I will list a few here and a few below what Ken wrote me about Lewis.

Ken:

 Has Harvard Law School degree but is not obnoxious about it. He is not obnoxious about anything.
 Is managing partner of splendid Lazy Hiker Brewing Company. You can find their beers in Athens.

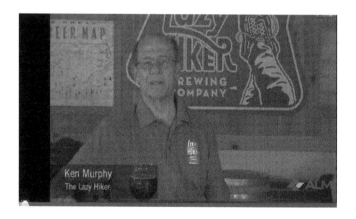

The rest can wait until after you read Ken's email. It was in response to my email inviting Ken and another hero to lodge with me during an upcoming event at the Athens house where Lewis once partied.

Ken's email:

Hey Pete!

Sounds like a great place, and it probably put you in the right mood for your book!

I'm not sure yet whether I'm going this year, but walking distance is key for me.

My grandfather and I shared a love for Grizzard's columns. In my first year of law school, back before we all had internet access, my grandfather sent me a weekly package with clippings of his columns of the past week. In my

law school dorm, folks would post
on their doors items that they
found interesting or read-worthy.
I shared a number of Grizzard's
columns this way and introduced
Grizzard to a lot of folks who had
never heard of him.

Wishing you the best on this
endeavor,
Ken

Continuing reasons why Ken is my
hero. For some reason Word will
not let me resume with reason
number "3".

Ken:

- Is the survivor of two organ
  transplants.
- Raises money for and
  awareness of organ donation.
- Was valedictorian of the 1978
  UGA class.
- Won the Wilkinson Award,
  making him the finest member

of Phi Gamma Delta on Planet Earth in 1978.

- Gave me his superb LP collection when he left for Harvard Law School. Or he sold them to me cheap.
- Was 1978 President of the UGA Business School Council and did not fire me as his Vice President.

That list could go on ad infinitum.

Ken was a sleeper in college. He was a bright and gentle guy with an easy smile and dry sense of humor. I liked Ken immensely, though about all we had in common was our fraternity and enrollment within the same college of business.

At the time I had no clue about Ken's latent brilliance. But enough about gushing on Ken. He is also modest, so this chapter will drive him nuts.

When Lewis wrote about or spoke of Yankees he did not follow the strict geographic definition. He referenced places like Chicago and Cleveland. True Yankees are from New England, maybe New York.

But Lewis did write about and speak of Ivy League people, and he did not do so fondly. He did not write much about lawyers that I am aware of, but I wish he did. I guess I must steal all lawyers jokes from my sons or the myriad of other lawyer loathing sources.

Yet as you can see, Ken succeeded in sharing the Gospel According to Lewis with future Ivy League lawyers. That speaks volumes about Ken's influence and universal appeal of the Gospel According to Lewis.

When Ken graduated from Harvard Law he clerked for a prestigious judge before a career of non-malicious corporate law. There he did not sue anyone I know, especially me. For that and so many other reasons, Ken remains my hero.

Plus, I just found out he loved Lewis Grizzard.

Postscript:

I must insist that people stop emailing me right after I finish writing their chapter. Ken responded to my request for consent to publish the first email.

Note that he calls it "filler". Nothing Ken has ever written in his remarkable life is filler. What did I say about Ken being modest?

Ken just informed me that he once considered buying or renting Lewis's former house. He would be that much more of my hero had he snagged it, but he did not.

I had to look up Doug Marlette to discover he was a political cartoonist. Not sure if I have the heart to tell Ken that Pat Conroy was partly responsible for Lewis not yet being inducted into the Georgia Writers Hall of Fame.

Maybe a 1978 UGA valedictorian can throw his weight around and help me get Lewis inducted. We shall see.

Ken's email:

Sure, not a problem if you need filler!

I went to look at Grizzard's house in Ansley Park when it went on the market, but I don't remember any

details. Among other reasons
(senioritis?), I wasn't in good
health at the time. Always thought
it would be cool to live there
though. Instead I lived in a house
that Doug Marlette lived in when
he won the Pulitzer; he often
invited Pat Conroy to visit so
Conroy's dogs could swim in the
pool!

Charity

Lewis is not necessarily recognized for charity work, but that does not mean we was not a charitable person.

Friends attest that he would do anything for you if he was able. Lewis spoke at banquets, appeared at events and even wrote pro bono on occasion if a friend asked.

Perhaps Lewis's earliest documented act of charity was taking in his father when he unexpectedly showed up on Lewis's college doorstep. His dad slept on Lewis's sofa for a period, eventually getting a job managing an Athens cafeteria. Lewis wrote that he was paid only in food his dad brought home, and the two of them ate far better than if either of them did the cooking. I know, this is family and perhaps should not be called charity, but we will come back to his dad later.

Lewis did not organize many if any charitable events, but he showed up to perform at a ton of them. In particular, golf tournaments. Lewis was an early celebrity participant in Scottish Rite Hospital tournaments, which later evolved into Egleston and Children's Healthcare Network events. If Lewis was announced to participate in a tournament, hundreds or thousands more spectators would attend.

Though others no doubt handled the details, Lewis was the marquee name at annual Smart Ass White Boys golf tournaments at Big Canoe. The name is derived from Atlanta Mayor Andrew Young's opinion of Walter Mondale campaign staffers. Lewis took a liking to the term and to Andy Young, who was invited to the tournaments and is said to have attended at least one. Not sure whether or not Ambassador Mayor Young played golf.

Another charity golf tournament was the annual Gator Hater in St. Simons or Sea Island the week before the annual Georgia Florida football game. The derivation of this name need not be explained to anyone but Yankees.

Perhaps the most prevalent expression of Lewis's charity was extended to those on "Lewis Scholarship". This was an informal designation regarding Lewis inviting people to events who could not afford to attend. These included bartenders and other friends of meager means who Lewis often invited to some of the golf tournaments above. If those friends said they could not afford the travel, or if Lewis simply knew they could not, he paid their expenses.

On New Year's Eve 1980 Lewis may have been charitable on two levels. In the French Quarter Lewis offered to sell a vendor's Lucky Dogs while the guy watched. The vendor declined, so Lewis bought/rented the whole stand and proceeded to sell or give away Lucky Dogs for the duration of the evening. If Lewis kept his receipts they likely went to either the Atlanta Constitution or Internal Revenue Service, so the price he may or may not have charged for Lucky Dogs is lost to the ages. If Lewis overpaid as was typical for the Lucky Dog stand, the vendor very likely considered it the act of charity of the year, decade or a lifetime.

A perhaps more obscure act of charity was when Lewis declined to cash checks payable to him for gambling debts. When he died dozens of such uncashed checks were found in his wallet, totaling tens of thousands of dollars. The makers of those checks were rarely in need of charity, but that is not the point.

If someone invited Lewis to an event there was a good chance he would speak, whether the host asked him to do so or not. One such occasion was the wedding weekend of a 'friend of a friend'. On short notice the remote acquaintance asked Lewis to say a few words at his rehearsal dinner. When Lewis asked what topic the guy wanted him to cover the groom to be said, "How about the sanctity of marriage?"

To which Lewis replied, "Are you sure? Isn't that like asking Idi Amin to speak at your pot luck dinner?"

For those too young to recall the name, Idi Amin was a despotic Ugandan dictator, rumored to be, among many very bad things, a cannibal.

Hosea Williams was known for feeding Atlanta's homeless and hungry around the holidays. Lewis and Hosea got into a snarky exchange about something, and one or the other proposed that they meet. Once they got together they bonded. I find no record of Hosea asking Lewis to serve meals. I speculate that had Hosea asked, Lewis would have served.

Coming full circle back to Lewis's father. Lewis Grizzard Sr. was indigent when he suffered a stroke in 1970. He languished in a Centerville GA hospital for weeks before dying, leaving an exorbitant bill. 24 year old Lewis Jr. quietly paid the entire bill.

Friends young and old attest that Lewis was generous to a fault. To paraphrase a president he liked to skewer, how you categorize Lewis's generosity depends on "what your definition of 'charity' is".

Saxby Chambliss

Several of Lewis's friends suggested I talk to Senator Saxby Chambliss. When I asked why, they advised he would have a few Lewis stories to tell. I then replied, "Great, but the Senator is now a busy attorney, and I gather he charges plenty for conversation even if I am not in need of legal assistance." Well, with proper introduction and the subject of Lewis Grizzard, some folks just like to talk.

I had met the Senator only once when he was not quite yet Senator, and I did not make the best of that opportunity. It was the November 30, 2002 Georgia vs Tech game, and my first visit to a game in Athens for over a decade. A friend got me access to the pre-game WSB Tailgate Show, then hosted from a makeshift studio under the Sanford Stadium bridge.

In my pre-call correspondence to the Senator I thought it wise to apologize in advance, as follows:

"Senator, I almost hope you do not remember the only time we met. It was at a UGA football pregame event. You had just been elected to the Senate but not yet sworn in. I had just returned to the south (Florida) for the first time since 1984. I was thrilled that you were elected but not a constituent. I greeted and congratulated you as, "Hello Mr. Governor". I corrected myself and said "Mr. Senator", but not until I wanted to crawl under a rock. That's my story, and I'm sticking to it."

The Senator's email reply was gracious and amiable, closing with:

"Don't worry, I have been called worse than Governor!"

At 16 minutes, my December 7 conversation with the Senator was the shortest of any I engaged in to write this book. The Senator got right to the point. He wanted to share a single experience that demonstrated Lewis's occasional inclination to want solitude and privacy.

Some 30 to 35 years earlier the Senator tailgated at a Georgia Florida game. As he stepped up to a portalet line he noticed Lewis a few folks in front of him. The Senator was not that recognizable in those days, but Lewis certainly was. And Lewis appeared that moment to wish he was not so recognizable.

Others in line and nearby lines cajoled Lewis to tell some stories. It took repeated

encouragement, yet Lewis rose to
the task. He launched into three
colorful narratives that had his
audience roaring. Then his
portalet opportunity arrived.
Lewis went in, did his business,
emerged and waved with a flourish
to all before quietly returning to
his tailgate companions.

This is also perhaps the least
outlandish and most family
friendly of all Lewis stories in
this book. Yet it is revealing.
Even if Lewis only wanted to make
a nature call undisturbed, his
celebrity made it difficult. Yet
he loved his admirers. When they
asked him to perform at even an
inopportune moment, he could not
let them down. Lewis performed.

In closing with the Senator I
brought up the name of a fine
Georgia Bulldog and his Moultrie
neighbor, Roy Reeves. I was Roy's
UGA Phi Gamma Delta pledge trainer

and claim full responsibility for
his considerable success in life.
The Senator joked in return that I
trained Roy well, as he is a
community leader and inspiration
on a number of levels.

Only weeks prior to our call
President Trump appointed Senator
Chambliss to his Intelligence
Advisory Board. I congratulated
the Senator and told him I feel
safer with him in that position. I
said if time allowed that as an
espionage buff I would like to ask
him questions he no doubt could
not answer. He replied:

"Oh, I could answer your
questions. But then I would have
to kill you."

Some punch lines are timeless.
They are even more timeless and
rewarding when delivered by such a
high achiever who has managed to
maintain a sense of humor

Funniest Man in America

Many proclaim Lewis Grizzard to be the funniest American who ever lived. I once thought so until I didn't. Now I think so again.

I can't quite remember when I first started reading Lewis Grizzard or when I first started to think he was funny. I thought I read him in high school, but then he was either writing serious or editing and not writing much at all. I am pretty certain I remember reading him at UGA and even passing around his columns at my fraternity house. But Lewis was in Chicago editing during some of those years and not writing much. We are talking the 1970s, and I may be talking flashbacks.

In late high school and early college I thought the funniest content on earth could be found in National Lampoon magazine. It

included a cover photo and
caption, "If You Don't Buy This
Magazine, We'll Kill This Dog". I
bought that and other magazines,
but not only to spare the quite
scared looking dog.

A funny writer and editor at
National Lampoon was P.J.
O'Rourke. He was partly
responsible for the 1974 epic,
"National Lampoon 1964 High School
Yearbook Parody". He was entirely
responsible for content within a
May 1976 edition "UNWANTED
FOREIGNERS". His piece within was
titled, "FOREIGNERS AROUND THE
WORLD" and subtitled, "A Brief
Survey of the Various Foreign
Types, Their Chief
Characteristics, Customs and
Manners". Important note: O'Rourke
used the Oxford comma. I do not.

I have read that P.J. O'Rourke
regrets that piece and would like
it pulled from circulation, where

it circulates only on the
secondary market. I am descended
from every nationality lampooned
by O'Rourke, and I thought it to
be the funniest English language
article ever written. There were
people who disagreed with me. I
knew a guy in college who ate
glass, and he found the article to
be offensive. Well, it was written
to offend every reader on the
planet. It succeeded, but only if
you did not have an extremely
perverse sense of humor.

Lewis Grizzard was politically
incorrect, knew how to stay barely
within boundaries and was never
ever profane. P.J. O'Rourke in
that piece threw all boundaries
and aversion to profanity down the
toilet. This was toilet humor at
its best or worst, depending on
perspective. I am still an
O'Rourke enthusiast.

Chasing still more rabbit holes while researching Lewis, I stumbled upon and subscribed to O'Rourke's American Consequences website. It is my intention to not explore that site until I finish this Lewis Grizzard book, or the year 2023, whichever comes soonest.

I also stumbled upon a 2010 video titled, "P.J. O'Rourke: The Funniest Man in America". The video lacks an introduction, and I can not figure out who his audience is. But since I was researching the funniest man in America I thought it worth a look.

Disclaimer: I do not think it was O'Rourke's intent to be hilarious in this speech. Thus, any blame can be directed at whoever wrote the title. People who write titles often do not look at content for which they add said title. Such people are either bad editors or their bad titling work escaped the attention of otherwise decent editors. Either way, it should not happen.

In the video O'Rourke is amusing in an intellectual way. I might call it humorously erudite. Erudite is a word many have to look up like I just did to make sure it was the exact word I wanted. It is not the exact word, but I use it just so you have to look it up.

Lewis Grizzard likely knew the word erudite very well without having to look it up. He was indeed erudite on many occasions on many topics, but that is not the first word most readers or audience members would use to describe what he wrote or said and what they read or heard. What most people said and many still say was and is simply this:

Lewis Grizzard was the funniest man in America.

A key issue is timelessness of humor. I would not dare republish O'Rourke's FOREIGNERS piece lest I get deported or shot by some intolerably intolerant humorless lunatic. I deem 95% of Lewis's work to be publishable today. Only rarely do I find a modern writer who proclaims Grizzard humor to be outdated, and drilling down on any writer who proclaims that inevitably reveals that writer to be humorless.

I myself got fired from a speaking gig for making an observation that the group to which I was to speak was led by almost 100% females. I even observed that to be a good thing with the comment, "Everyone knows women do everything better than men." The result was I got fired. If I ever meet the person who fired me, I expect I will find them to be humorless. I will further wager they would not like what Lewis wrote. Their loss.

I expect P.J. O'Rourke got a handsome honorarium to speak to whoever the audience was in that video. I wonder if they sent FOREIGNERS out a week before that speech if they would have canned him.

Lewis's physician recently told me Lewis spoke to an international group of cardiologists in Orlando. The MD asserts that audience members from every continent present roared and proclaimed it to be the best and funniest speech they had ever heard. Of course Lewis was a cardiology expert from the consumer's perspective, so that may have helped frame his talk.

Had Lewis lived to be P.J. O'Rourke's current age of 71

perhaps he would have become more conspicuously erudite. I wish the world had a chance to find out.

Thriving on Chaos

Lewis Grizzard once said that writing a daily column is like being married to a nymphomaniac. The first two weeks is fun.

Actually a 1990 New York Times article said Lewis said someone else once said it. But I can't find who that someone else is, so I give all credit to Lewis.

That quote may be true if you began writing columns in grade school like Lewis did. But if you begin writing at age 60+ like I did, you will never ever run out of stuff to write about.

Last week I had coffee with a friend of Lewis who said he looked forward to something going wrong in his life because he needed material. A missed plane, bad hotel or stepping in something

warm and steamy on the sidewalk
could fuel him for a week.

In other words, Lewis thrived on
chaos.

Lord knows I have experienced
enough chaos in the last two years
to last most people a lifetime.
Let's take one example. My house
sank.

No, my basement did not flood.
Well, yes it did. But when most
people's basement floods the house
stays put. Mine did not. It sank.
Because I lived on a houseboat.

Lewis would have loved living on a
houseboat, but he would have done
it at Lake Oconee, not my chosen
Lake Lanier.

I chose a houseboat and Lake
Lanier to share unique experiences
with my two teenage sons, for whom
I enjoy joint custody. The boys

actually selected the houseboat from three finalists. To my surprise they chose the oldest and cheapest without a second thought, and that was okay by me. It was like a three bedroom 1.5 bath Holiday Inn suite, but with a far better view than a parking lot dumpster.

The boys earned lifetime boater safety certifications, which makes them better boaters than 137% of all boaters on Lake Lanier, particularly on holiday weekends. We had movies nights on the flybridge under the stars, and the lone fisherman among us caught bass, catfish and carp. We had friends and cousins join us for tubing and wakeboarding and had a blast.

More than once I was threatened with eviction from the best marina on Lake Lanier for living on a houseboat, which is a Corps of

Engineers violation that only my
marina takes seriously. I can name
four other marinas that turn a
blind eye to it.

You can't even get the Corps to
define "living on a houseboat",
because I asked. Repeatedly. Once
they said one also needs a brick
and mortar address. I had that, as
shown on my slip lease agreement.
Then they said time on a boat must
be for pleasure and leisure, not
for residence or work. That begged
the question, what if I derive
pleasure leisurely residing and
working on a boat.

Best not to toy with the Corps of
Engineers or the excellent marina
that answers to them, especially
if your boat will one day sink.

The boat sank due to a flooded
basement. The basement, pronounced
"h-u-l-l" to nautical types,
flooded due to a leaky water

heater valve. It took weeks to
discover that was the cause
because we could not research such
matters until the vessel was
brought afloat and hauled to a
storage yard for inspection and
restoration.

Suffice it to say, that experience
caused more than a little chaos in
my life. I was even ¾ of the way
through writing my first book,
Road to Water, about how I chose
to live on a houseboat and the
pure joy of it in between eviction
notices. Only when I had to part
with the boat due to unsalvageable
engines that we thought we had
salvaged did I stop writing the
book.

What was going to be a happy
ending became unhappy, and I hate
sob stories. Many on Lake Lanier
followed my plight, offered me
encouragement, referred me to
essential vendors and even vowed

they would buy my book. As it is,
I am for the time being known as
the sad guy who sank arguably the
largest vessel to ever sink on
Lake Lanier.

So, that led to some homelessness,
work disruption and other chaos
that in my opinion far surpassed
Lewis level chaos of a missed
plane, bad hotel or stepping in
something warm and steamy on the
sidewalk. When I stepped into
something I sank up to my neck.
And I am still working to scrape
it off.

Perhaps the saddest aspect about
that boat is that I had renamed it
from "Volaritaville" to "Dawg.
House. Boat.". It had once resided
on the Tennessee River and been
used at Vol Navy weekends. I had
replaced the wretched early
graphics with beautiful new ones
that brought a smile to everyone I
cared about. There was still some

residual Vol stench on the interior, but post sinkage lake water took care of that.

Unfortunately nothing could take care of dead engines and a more than exhausted insurance policy.

I aspire to own that boat again or one like it. To achieve that I must write lots of books and columns and avoid marrying a nymphomaniac.

If I do marry a nymphomaniac it will help if she types faster than I do, can file my chaotic notes and make strong coffee. Best also if she is not from Dayton Ohio and shaves her legs. Is that too much to ask?

More on Lewis's encounter with an unshaven legged woman from Dayton Ohio in a future column if I find my notes.

Brushes With Lewis

This all makes me very nervous. But it happened, I've told a few important people about it, and they say I should confess it.

For over 4 decades people have sporadically referenced Lewis Grizzard about my writing. I would never dare say it. Other people did. But only about once every decade.

It all makes me very nervous.

Months ago a childhood buddy with whom I first remember swapping Lewis clippings mentioned that I was editor of our 1968 grade school newspaper. I have zero recollection of that. Yet he sent me a grainy photo of the mimeograph front page as evidence. Lewis was not even a topic of our phone conversation, but it was a Lewis enthusiast who had to remind

me when my writing "career" began.
Separately, in recent weeks I
learned Lewis wrote during grade
school for the Newnan newspaper
about little league games in which
he played. Yes, Lewis wrote for a
higher level publication than I
did, but I do not remember writing
for anyone.

Lewis wrote about his fear of
flunking English 101 at the
University of Georgia during his
freshman year.

Fast forward to my 1976 UGA
English 101. I may have had
Lewis's teacher. He was 11 years
older than me. This teacher was
one of those jet black haired
steely women who could have been
50 or 80.

She was generally known for
preventing freshmen from becoming
sophomores. One day she asked me
to stay after class. I feared I

might be driving home in my VW Beetle that afternoon. She asked, "Do you know who Lewis Grizzard is?" I replied that I sure did and asked why. She did not answer directly but instead suggested that I become a writer. I did not connect the dots she tried to help me connect. I told her I was a business school marketing major and did not want to switch to journalism. One can not be a whole lot more obtuse than I was that day. I do not recall the rest of the conversation. I did manage to become a sophomore.

Fast forward to 1983. I was convention manager for an Atlanta division of Siemens, who few in the US had heard of back then. I wrote two documents that day. The first was my two week notice of resignation, as I had accepted a job in Chicago. The second was a site inspection report for a board meeting I would not be around to manage. Since I was a lame duck with nothing to lose, I got a little cheeky in the memo to the president. To paraphrase, "You asked me to find the best resort in Cancun, and I did. It is a Hyatt, but it is a Hyatt with potholes on the tennis courts and sinkholes on the golf course. Hyatt staff said that will all be fixed, but I would take that with a grain of salt. Plus a shot of tequila. I sincerely wish I could help prepare everything for your meeting, but by then I will be in Chicago working for someone else. I do strongly recommend that my successor go in a few days early to help fill in those potholes and sinkholes."

The president called me to his office at the end of the day. "First, I regret to see you are leaving us. Second, how did you get Lewis Grizzard to write this damn memo?" He was kidding, but I thought it eerie. I consciously attempted to channel Lewis in that second document. He went on to ask if I was serious about the property conditions. I was. He sheepishly confessed that he should have heeded my recommendations of more predictable US destinations like Orlando. Cancun was his idea, yet his 25 year old meeting guy was right. I did not say this but wish I had. "Lewis Grizzard would have picked Cancun too."

Fast forward to the 1990s. I had married an Auburn girl - Lewis would say a big mistake - but on trips to Atlanta we often stayed at her parents' house in the suburbs. Her dad was among the most fanatical Grizzard enthusiasts who ever lived. And he was a Michigan born Norwegian! On the stand in the guest bathroom was a rotating stack of Grizzard books. As soon as it was available

to be framed the famous cartoon
showing Catfish welcoming Lewis at
the Pearly Gates went on the
hallway wall outside of that
bathroom.

I did have the image in this
chapter but could not figure out
who owns the copyright. Google
"lewis at the pearly gates" to see
it. The image still adorns home
and office walls of many I
interviewed for this book.

I wrote annual Christmas letters
that satirized dull, sanctimonious
holiday letters. Upon check in at
the in-laws' house pop-in-law
often greeted me with that letter
in hand, a grin and a hug. Once or
twice he said my letters reminded
him of Grizzard. I divorced his
daughter after 25 years of
marriage in 2014. I once loved
her, but I still love her late
father. What would Lewis do with
that?

Fast forward to 2017. I wrote a
press release for only my second
paying client, a very prominent
UGA business school alumna. We
were trying to sell her excellent
autobiography.

Afterward the alum volunteered,
"You. Are. Good. Ok wow, I'm so
impressed. You write like Lewis
Grizzard. You are witty, sharp, a
little acerbic, and compelling."
To say I was floored would be an
understatement. My goal was to
make her book a bestseller, as it
still should be. That effort got
sidetracked when she accepted the
job as CEO of the AT&T Performing
Arts Center in Dallas.

That ends of my eerie references
to Lewis Grizzard. And I must
again apologize to editors for
exceeding 800 words. This stands
at 941 words. I gotta cut down on
caffeine

BBQ Bible

Like Lewis Grizzard, I love BBQ.
Or barbecue if you feel the need
to spell it out. I once aspired to
take the Lewis Grizzard Georgia
BBQ road trip. I don't think Lewis
ever mapped out such a thing, but
a BBQ loving friend once did.
Unfortunately I can no longer find
either the map or the friend.

As stated in a recent column,
Google "lewis grizzard lake
lanier", and the top result will
be a 2017 article I wrote about
Smoky Q, a Lanier BBQ joint Lewis
would have loved. It turns out no
one should really Google "lewis
grizzard lake lanier" because
Lewis was a Lake Oconee guy. More
on Lake Oconee BBQ shortly.

Long ago I did make it to many BBQ
joints on the Lewis BBQ tour map
that I since lost. All were
exceptional in my opinion, with

the exception of Lewis's supposed favorite close to his hometown. I will not name it, but many will know what and where it is. The day I went decades ago it did not appeal, and I will leave it at that. Tens of thousands still swear by the place.

I wish I could remember the names of all the stellar places where I followed Lewis's lead, but I can't because those too were decades ago. One was Brinson's in Millen. It is in fact a great reason to travel to Millen, even though that town may or may not be responsible for burdening the world with Millenials.

Lewis had certain BBQ idiosyncrasies I still conform to not because I necessarily agree, but only because Lewis articulated them to be BBQ offenses. The first is that beef is not BBQ. I have had some knock down drag out good

beef smoked and seasoned with
excellent flavorings and sauce
that might resemble a certain word
to certain people west of Georgia.
But I won't call it BBQ. Or even
barbecue. Dang good tasting
brisket is what it is.

Just one more Lewis idiosyncrasy,
then I will press on. You don't
put coleslaw on top of BBQ. If
people swear not to tell anyone, I
did that once, and it did not kill
me. I even thought to perhaps do
it again. But no.

This all brings us back to Lake
Oconee and a BBQ place where Lewis
did in fact eat often, but I had
yet to get there until December
13, 2018. My visit had to do with
the newspaperman largely
responsible for Lewis being at
Lake Oconee in the first place. We
are talking Carey Williams of the
Greensboro Herald Journal, and

Holcomb's Bar B Que, conveniently also in Greensboro.

I am not certain if Lewis objected to the Bar B Que spelling vs BBQ or barbecue. It did not stop him from eating there often, so I will not obsess about it. Carey Williams was my host for both two hours of Lewis conversation and lunch at Holcomb's Bar B Que.

If that guy I can't find with the Lewis Grizzard Georgia BBQ road trip map did not have Holcomb's on that map, he should have. One minor snag is that no one currently at Holcomb's ever met Lewis. There was once a Lewis photo on the wall. It is gone now, and no one knows where it is. That's the decline of Lewis's legacy my biography will hopefully at least begin to reverse.

Now, on to Holcomb's food. I always get nervous when entering a

BBQ shrine lest I order the wrong thing. Carey solved that with, "Give us two plates." I fully believed food would be included with those plates, and indeed it was. Knock down drag out good food. Three staples. Chopped pork. Brunswick stew. Cole Slaw.

Side basket of white bread. Carey had sweet tea. I had a Co-Cola. Don't tell anyone, but tea is one food stuff I can not tolerate, hot or cold, sweet or not.

Then came some decisions. Put sauce on the pork or not. I always say try the pork first without sauce. I did. It was best without sauce. Then Carey said the sauce is good, so I put a little on. It was better with sauce. Then I tried another bite without sauce, and that was better. If you see where this is going tell me, because I have no idea. I must go back to figure it out.

The Brunswick stew was like manna from the Gods, as was the cole slaw. I dared not put the manna cole slaw on the manna pork for fear Carey might send a memo up to Lewis. Carey left a little food on his plate. It was all I could do to keep from breaching Greensboro etiquette and ask to take my host's leftovers home in a to go box. I have no qualms about taking strangers' leftovers home when I am paying. Which I wasn't.

Holcomb's ranks up there with Smokey Q which ranks up there with Brinson's. That is to say 12 on a scale of 10. No one is better than another, but you must go to all three before you die. You could do no better than to actually die eating at any one of the three.

One edge Holcomb's had going over the other two is a guy came over to say hi to Carey. He was Kirby

Smart's roommate at UGA. If one of Kirby's roommates ever ate at Smoky Q or Brinson's while I was there I was too busy eating or eyeing strangers' leftovers to notice.

Dang it. Over the 800 word column maximum again. This now totals 952 words. Sorry editors. I blame Carey.

Dr. Randy Martin

As the world knows Lewis Grizzard was not a healthy man during the last few years of his life. During that time no one was closer to Lewis on a daily basis than his cardiac physician, Dr. Randy Martin.

Now a world renowned expert on many things related to the heart, in 1993 young Dr. Martin had already accomplished much. He had served on faculty and staff at Stanford, the University of Virginia, the Mayo Medical School and Mayo Clinic. He had a chance to put all that training to good use when he met Lewis.

Following his 1985 surgery resulting from infected wisdom teeth, Lewis had plugged along as his usual Lewis self. Hard work and play, hard drinking and smoking. That would soon considerably slow down by necessity. Lewis's first replacement valve was famously from a pig. His second implanted in 85 might have been as well, but that is not the point. It was shot, as was much of Lewis's heart. Again.

Lewis has famously been called the writer from hell, guest speaker from hell and many things from hell. And many people who called Lewis that liked him. At Emory Lewis was known as the patient from hell, yet fewer liked him. Few wanted to deal with Lewis the patient ever again. This brings us to Randy Martin, MD.

After meeting in Emory's emergency room, Dr. Martin and Lewis hit it off. Perhaps Lewis had mellowed, perhaps it was Dr. Martin's bedside manner, perhaps a combination of both. This time around, for whatever reason, Lewis was not the patient from hell. That was a good thing because he needed a lot of time at Emory to restore some semblance of health before they could even perform surgery.

By all accounts, Lewis should not have survived his third surgery. He was in a medically induced coma for several weeks, and physicians were uncertain if he would ever emerge with his faculties intact. One afternoon Dr. Martin and a couple of staff were at Lewis's ICU bedside chatting. They were each trying to remember the name of the comedian whose shtick was always being tipsy. No one could come up with it. Then, with tubes coming out of every orifice from the neck up, Lewis gurgled his first post surgical words:

"Foschtew Bwookths!" Or Foster Brooks. Lewis was back.

With all this Dr. Martin had
several new mandates for Lewis.
Drink less. Eat better. Rest more.
Stay away from people who are bad
influences. Quit smoking. No
telling how many of these Lewis
took to heart.

With prolonged unconsciousness
comes other complications, one of
which is limited blood circulation
to extremities. Lewis's left index
finger was disabled to the point
they consulted a plastic surgeon
to amputate. After weighing that
option Lewis declined. He wanted
what remained of his digits to
remain intact, for better or for
worse.

It is reported Lewis received
50,000 get well letters while at
Emory. Dr. Martin can attest as an
eye witness that a busload of fans
arrived from Alabama, pulled up to
a curb on Clifton Road, got out,
unfurled a banner that said "Get

Well Lewis!!!", applauded
themselves and him, then got back
on the bus and returned to
Alabama.

Lewis convalesced for 4 to 6 weeks
at Emory, then moved to his
girlfriend's apartment to
convalesce some more. Shortly
thereafter a blood clot moved to
his liver. The result was that his
liver stretched, likely causing
far more pain than Lewis had ever
endured in his life. Lewis
soldiered through it. What choice
did he have?

Over the course of weeks and
months to follow Lewis was in and
out of Emory. Dr. Martin and Lewis
spent a lot of time together both
there and wherever Lewis went,
more often than not, 'off the
clock' for Dr. Martin. By this
time they were not doctor and
patient. They were friends. Dr.
Martin took the opportunity to

prepare Lewis's spiritual self with the comment, "My friend, if you don't believe in the power of prayer now, you never will. I certainly do." Only Lewis and God can say for certain, but Dr. Martin is confident Lewis found badly needed peace in his final year.

Which is not to say Lewis became some altar boy. During one stint at Emory he emerged after 'smoking in the boy's room', having singed a towel in his failed attempt to conceal evidence. During that or another stint Dr. Martin helped Lewis break Emory rules. Lewis said he pined for a hot dog, and Dr. Martin had Varsity dogs delivered courtesy of an accomplice, Lewis's driver James Shannon. The doctor figured a dog or two would kill Lewis no faster than bland hospital food. Don't we all wish we had common sense doctors like that?

Another time Dr. Martin was complicit in the violation of a far more strictly enforced Emory rule. Dr. Martin asked Lewis if there was anything at all he could get to comfort Lewis. Lewis replied, "Yes, but you can't do it. I miss Catfish and would love to see him." Again, Dr. Martin dispatched driver James as partner in crime.

Catfish arrived at the laundry entrance during the wee hours when the area would likely be unstaffed. They placed Catfish in a laundry gurney and covered him in sheets and towels. All went smoothly until they got close to Lewis's door, whereupon Catfish barked. No matter how accomplished one is as a physician, everyone knows head nurses are in charge when it comes to activities on their ward. Catfish was ordered out of the facility and off the premises - STAT. Lewis licks on the face, at least from Catfish, would have to wait until he was discharged.

Months passed, and Lewis came and went back and forth to Emory as he strengthened and weakened off and on. Lewis was living on borrowed time, and he knew it.

Then came the hospital stay from which Lewis would never be discharged. Troops from near and far rallied and prepared for what all suspected to be the inevitable. Lewis got affairs in order and made preparations. Dr. Martin was given power of attorney to exercise Lewis's wishes.

In a well documented visit with his physicians Lewis was advised he had what has been recorded as "less than a 50% chance" of surviving his 4th surgery. Dr. Martin would not put a percentage on it, but less than 50% was an optimistic exaggeration. In the room were three of the most renowned heart doctors in the world, Ellis Jones, Robert Guyton and Randy Martin. When one of them asked if he had any questions, Lewis replied, "When is the next bus to Albuquerque?"

One of the three physicians was not the humorous sort, and the line flew over his head. It was not Dr. Martin, who had come to expect as much from Lewis. The doctor who did not get the joke may have wondered if Lewis thought there might be better heart specialists in New Mexico. That will be a question for others to answer.

Lewis married for a 4th time. I know for certain several people were there that day, though not necessarily in the room for the ceremony. Ernie Cain served as one of two best men. Lewis apologized for having two. He either forgot or thought it good to have a backup. Ernie helped lift Lewis out of his wheelchair to take his vows. I do not know who was best man #2.

Also present that day were Jim Minter, Ludlow Porch, and James Shannon. Maybe Shelton Stevens.

When Lewis emerged from surgery, after a passage of time it was obvious there was no brain activity. Dr. Martin allowed 10 or so friends to say their last farewells before following Lewis's wish and allowing him to pass away.

Dr. Martin asserts that Lewis was the most "medically tough" patient he has ever had. Lewis endured ventricular assist devices, heart assist machines and other invasive contraptions that cause considerable discomfort. Lewis bore a strong constitution and courageous demeanor, the likes of which Dr. Martin has never seen. All the while and until the end, he somehow maintained a sense of humor.

Speaking of humor, Dr. Martin asserts that Lewis was without question the funniest person he has ever known. At his invitation Lewis spoke at an international cardiology convention in Orlando. That had to have taken some courage on the part of Dr. Martin, as there would be no telling what Lewis might say on his farewell tour with nothing to lose and a room full of people, the likes of whom he ridiculed for not keeping current magazines in their lobbies. As in Time magazines with Roosevelt on the cover. Teddy.

Dr. Martin reports that Lewis had the world's top MDs from six continents howling and attesting it was the best speech they ever heard. No telling if they ordered newer waiting room magazines as a result.

Epilogue

Decades ago there were bumper stickers that read:

"Honk if you have been married to Lewis Grizzard."

I have spoken to many who saw them and a few who adorned their bumper with one. If you have one please let me know.

I hereby pledge to launch a bumper sticker to read:

"Honk if you have a great Lewis Grizzard story and got left out of Peter Stoddard's first book."

That's kinda wordy and might be hard to read. I'll sweat those details later.

There will be more Lewis Grizzard stories to follow. If you have one

to share I want to hear it. Thank
you!

Peter Stoddard
stoddardmedia@gmail.com

About the Author

Peter Stoddard graduated from the University of Georgia with a Bachelor of Business Administration degree in Marketing.

His first job was as North American Convention Manager for Atlanta's Lanier Business Products. Lanier made insanely expensive dictation and word processing equipment that their account executives on steroids sold like banshees. Today your phone does what Lanier products did.

Peter's second job was as North American Convention Manager for an Atlanta division of Siemens, a company no one in America had yet heard of. Peter's friends thought he traveled the continent promoting Seagram's, and their confusion was okay with him. It even attracted babes.

Peter then took a sales job in Chicago with a company that offered convention center labor less likely to kill their client than convention center labor that had previously been available. It took a deft degree of humor to not get killed at that profession, especially in Chicago.

All this time Peter had to write well, or at least try to. If he wrote poorly his employers would look very bad and/or someone might get hurt or killed.

Then Peter became a real estate agent and later a broker in the Redneck Riviera resort market of Northwest Florida. There he represented some customers who made a killing and others who got killed. Figuratively of course, with the occasional exception of rip currents and bad oysters.

As a real estate guy Peter wrote innovative Email Bulletins talking about how the Redneck Riviera was transitioning from the bucolic Best Kept Secret of the South into a New Urbanism mecca a/k/a hoity toity haven for arrogant rich people. He did not write the bulletins quite like that of course, as more and more of his customers were arrogant rich people. Still, that transformation is why Peter moved back to Atlanta.

In 2017 Peter founded Stoddard Media, a Public Relations writing business. In his first year a client nominated him for Forsyth County Public Relations & Marketing Firm of the Year. Peter did not win because he refused to buy an ad larger than a competitor's ad at the top of the ballot. Having lived in Chicago for so long Peter regrets not getting dead people to vote for him.

In late 2018 Peter began researching why the legacy of his favorite humor writer seemed to be fading. That writer is Lewis Grizzard, and Peter found his way into the homes and offices of people who knew Lewis well and had dang humorous stories to tell that the world had not heard. Peter took it upon himself to tell those stories in a way he hoped would make Lewis proud. Lewis deserves better than a fading legacy.

Which brings us to this book. Lewis Grizzard used to comment that if you did not like his column do not complain. The newspaper in which the column appeared cost 25 cents. Adjusted for inflation that would be about $1,723.69. If that is off it is because Peter was a Marketing major and not a Finance major. This eBook runs $9.95. A bargain any way you look at it. We hope you will agree.

Appendix

I wish I could offer an appendix,
yet that would take decades to
prepare. Please pretend I am
simply recovering from an arduous
and painful appendectomy.

Back Cover

This was a faux back cover for the eBook, so we left it in.

This is a hotel meeting room in Newnan Georgia. Lewis went to Newnan High School. The front desk person did not know who Lewis is.

That makes me sad. Plus, the Grizzard room should never be vacant. But perhaps I ask too much.

Even in the town where Lewis should be familiarly remembered, some do not remember him.

Thankfully, to counter that I heard from so many who passed Lewis's works down to their children and grandchildren.

Whether you read everything Lewis ever wrote or have never heard of the guy, we hope you will enjoy the amazing stories shared by those who knew Lewis well.

For decades Lewis brought a smile to folks across the country while they enjoyed their morning coffee. This is our best effort to honor him with a few more smiles.

Sit back and enjoy Lewis "stuff" as told by friends who loved him. We promise you will learn at least 10 facts about him you never knew. Maybe 30 or even 50 facts.

Or your money back. But to get your money back you will have to prove you knew facts before

reading the book. That could be
tricky.

Best to ignore any money back
guarantee until we figure out how
that might work.

The End

Books should end in an even page number.

Made in the USA
Columbia, SC
20 April 2020

93110630R00263